365

FAMILY
GAMES
AND
PASTIMES

Martin and Simon Toseland are brothers who decided a few years ago
that they could test the limits of fraternal existence by writing together.
For this collection they have researched games and pastimes dating
back hundreds of years.

365

FAMILY
GAMES
AND
PASTIMES

MARTIN & SIMON
TOSELAND

◨ SQUARE PEG

Published by Square Peg 2012

2 4 6 8 10 9 7 5 3 1

Copyright © Martin & Simon Toseland 2010
Illustration copyright © Square Peg 2010
Illustrations by Eleanor Crow
Design by Friederike Huber

First published in Great Britain in 2010 by
Square Peg
Random House, 20 Vauxhall Bridge Road,
London SW1V 2SA

www.vintage-books.co.uk

Addresses for companies within The Random House Group Limited can be found at:
www.randomhouse.co.uk/offices.htm

The Random House Group Limited Reg. No. 954009

A CIP catalogue record for this book
is available from the British Library

ISBN 9780224086554

The Random House Group Limited supports The Forest Stewardship Council (FSC®),
the leading international forest certification organisation. Our books carrying the FSC label
are printed on FSC® certified paper. FSC is the only forest certification scheme endorsed
by the leading environmental organisations, including Greenpeace. Our paper procurement
policy can be found at www.randomhouse.co.uk/environment

Mixed Sources
Product group from well-managed
forests and other controlled sources
www.fsc.org Cert no. TT-COC-2139
© 1996 Forest Stewardship Council
FSC

Printed and bound by CPI Group (UK) Ltd, Croydon, CR0 4YY

To five generations of strong and funny women who are,
or were, great at making the rules and winning the games –

Daisy, Joan, Kim, Hannah and Maisie the dog

CONTENTS

Introduction

This book is intended to bring a little joy to your life at any time of the year. It's a celebration of the games and pastimes we've played and enjoyed throughout our lives, as well as some which we'd forgotten about, and many which we've discovered in the course of our research.

It has been partly inspired by childhood memories of staying with our maternal grandmother, Daisy, who ran the local 'shop' in a Lincolnshire village. This shop was a magical place to us, with row after row of old-fashioned sweet jars lined up behind the wooden counter, their contents waiting to be measured out on the old brass scales or sneakily removed by hand when no one was around – somehow Daisy always knew when we had done this.

In the evening, the shop became the local pub, and farmers and neighbours would sit on wooden stools on the flagstone floors, telling each other stories, playing cards and entertaining us with jokes and simple tricks. The warm light and flickering shadows cast by oil lamps reinforced the sense that this all happened more than a lifetime ago. Now we look back, it was like a rustic scene from a Victorian costume drama.

These experiences rooted games firmly in our lives. Sitting at the dining table, we played endless word games like Footballers' Initials and Capitals (page 105) with our parents. No one ever seemed to tire of playing, and there was nothing dainty or overbearing about it. It was really just communication and shared enjoyment.

When travelling on holiday, we would play games in the car – I-Spy and guessing games – to take our minds off the sun-baked seats and seemingly endless journeys. At Christmas, when Daisy invariably came to stay, we played hands of cards until late into the night – Newmarket, Nap, Draw the World Dry (as we used to call it). We, and Daisy, loved the excitement, the tension of winning the jackpot or getting all the money bet on a 'horse'.

Later, we'd play games with friends met on holidays, on long rainy days in a beachside bar when we were bored of listening to personal stereos or reading books, and craved some human company. Because that's what games and pastimes are really all about. They're a great way of getting to know other people – they break down barriers and give an instant shared language and common goal. They make it easy for people to get along, assuming you can rein in your

competitive instincts. And then, suddenly, you're playing games
with children again – your own, your nephews and nieces, those
in other families.

It's claimed that no one plays games any more, that we've all
become isolated from each other by TV, computers and mobile
phones. We think this is a myth – there never was and never will be
a Golden Age, and things simply change. Of course you're not going
to make a walkie-talkie out of string and tin cans when you can text
your friend in the garden.

Having said that, there is charm and simplicity in a lot of these old
activities which bear rediscovery. There would be no harm, we felt,
in collecting some of our favourite games – party games, ball games,
card games, magic tricks, drinking games, memory games – to make
them accessible to everyone.

While we were researching, we realised that there's also a whole
world of games that had passed us by – many consigned to books
long out of print and destined to be forgotten for ever unless
we gave them a fighting chance. So we've included lots of old
games and pastimes from the earlier part of last century, back to
Victorian days and beyond, simply because we thought they might
be enjoyed.

We've also tried to stick with games and pastimes which are
practical, easy to learn and require a minimum of equipment. The
idea is that you can open the book at nearly any page and find
something to do, without having to go on an expensive shopping
trip. So cards, glue, paper, pens, dice and a cricket bat are among the
more complicated equipment needed to enjoy this book. With any
luck you'll have some, or all, of those items shoved in the back of a
cupboard somewhere.

There are games and pastimes for every occasion, whether that be
a snowy February weekend or a hot July afternoon. The activities
are loosely grouped by season, but most of the games can be played
at any time of year. There are things to do on trains, in cars, at
the seaside, in the countryside and, of course, in every room of the
house. There are activities for all ages too – many of the games were
created for children but there are definitely some which we'd rather
they didn't attempt.

Where possible we've included more information than you might
get in a straight compendium of games – be it some history or the
origins of a word or phrase or even mentions in literature – just to

give the sense that many of these games have been with us for a very long time.

Talking of which, we did, in the course of our research, come across some games, once popular, which looked great but which we felt obliged to exclude on modern health and safety grounds or, occasionally, on the grounds of questionable taste. They are, nevertheless, a fascinating insight into what was, and no longer is, generally considered acceptable as entertainment.

Bigamy, for instance, is a party game from the 1930s which involves men chasing after an extra wife. Or Babes in the Wood which requires a 'wicked uncle' to search for a couple of children who must, when discovered, run home for dear life before he touches one of them. And Ancient Britons, another children's game, where the 'husband' must hunt enemies to bring 'home' to his wife. She then stands guard over them while he goes off to hunt more.

Some of the old scouting games we found were borderline dangerous and, with names like Baiting the Badger and Cock Fighting, we thought their appeal might be limited.

Our favourite game not to make it into this selection is the ancient sport of rhubarb thrashing. We'll give you the rules, just in case you think we misjudged. A couple of blindfolded idiots stand in dustbins facing each other and then thrash each other with sticks of rhubarb until one gives in. Well, maybe it's due a comeback – we never did much like rhubarb.

Anyway, we hope you enjoy using this book as much as we've enjoyed researching and writing it. Let the games commence, as someone once said.

Martin and Simon Toseland

CHILDREN'S PARTY GAMES

Parties map the course of a child's life – from pre-school gatherings to birthday celebrations – and most parties benefit from the inclusion of games. They're a good way to get children mixing and to allow them to run off some steam. Like most people, some of our earliest memories are of the games we used to play at parties, and these stay with you for the rest of your life. What follows is a selection of some of our favourites, starting with a few that break the ice, moving on to more boisterous games and ending with ones to calm everyone down before home time. There's something here for everyone. Let's party!

Let's Get this Party Started!

At a lot of children's parties there may be some guests who don't know most of the other people and will be very shy about joining in. The last thing you want is for these poor souls to be feeling left out, so to start with here are a few games to get things going.

Famous Pairs

This needs a little advance preparation, and some sticky labels.

Before the party, draw up a list of famous pairings, from books, real life, cinema, historical figures and so on. You might choose, for example, a book theme with Tom Sawyer and Huckleberry Finn, or Harry Potter and Ron Weasley, for younger players, or a celebrity theme with Hillary and Bill Clinton, Camilla and Charles, or Angelina Jolie and Brad Pitt, for the teenage children and grown-ups.

As guests arrive, each has a sticker with one name stuck to their back. As they mingle, they ask questions which may only be answered with a yes or a no, in order first to work out who they are, and then find the other half of their pair.

Crazy Hunt

This game takes a bit of preparation before the guests arrive.

The idea is simply to put twenty familiar objects in unusual places. You can confine this to one room or, if you don't mind guests straying further, widen the search area to the whole house. Each guest is then given a pen and paper and allocated an amount of time to try to guess which are the twenty out-of-place objects – a bicycle pump in the bath, a pair of underpants on a plant, a toothbrush in the sugar bowl, and so on. The winner is the person who has found the most objects in the given time (unless someone has managed to find them all).

Wool Gatherers

Cut up about thirty lengths of wool of four different colours – say brown, blue, red and green – and distribute them in various places around the room. On lamps, plants, the television and so on.

At a given signal, tell the children to go wool gathering, and collect as many lengths of wool as they can find.

After a short length of time, shout 'Stop'. The children count their wool and you tell them that brown scores four points, green three points, red two points and blue one point.

The child with the highest total wins a sweet or chocolate.

Simon Says

Another very old classic game – the fun is to be had in giving rapid-fire instructions to catch players out. Can be played by all ages, but especially good for younger children.

A grown-up, Simon, stands in front of the players and gives a series of rapid orders: 'Simon says put your hands up – hop on one leg – touch your nose.' And so on.

Players follow Simon's instructions precisely.

However, if Simon says simply, 'Clap your hands,' i.e. The instruction is not preceded by 'Simon says', they must stand completely still and make no move.

If any player forgets, and performs the order anyway, they are out, or pay a forfeit.

Follow My Leader

This is a great game for very young children. It needs no special equipment and is one of the easiest games as it can be played practically anywhere, but is most fun in a big space, or outdoors, where movement is unrestricted.

One player is made leader and the other players all follow by doing exactly what the leader does.

You may decide to limit the number of actions so, for instance, the leader may only use his hands, or legs, or voice. Or it may be a game in which all of these actions are combined. It can be made into a contest by having one player act as judge and decide who was last to perform an action, or who failed to perform it properly. These players can then be marked out of the game until a winner is found.

Sweet Straws

This is a game for children, though we know plenty of grown-ups who would happily participate.

Each player should have a straw and two pudding bowls or plates. Fill one of every person's bowls with an equal number of small sweets like Smarties, though not so small that they might get stuck in the straw.

On a given signal, the players should suck the sweets onto the end of their straw and let them drop into the other, empty bowl. The first player to transfer all the sweets from one bowl to the other is the winner. Whether they get to eat all their sweets should be decided beforehand.

Alternatively, you could set a time limit of, say, one minute, at which point all the players can keep the number of sweets they've accumulated. This way, it doesn't matter so much if the number of sweets in each bowl is slightly uneven.

Bake a Pie

A game for younger children which tests their memory and attention.

A grown-up is the cook and all the children are the ingredients. The cook tells each child which ingredient they are – butter, flour, water, sugar, and so on.

The cook stands in front of them, mimes as if he or she is making the pie, and calls out the ingredients.

When a child's nominated ingredient is mentioned, that child must step forward.

The cook should try to distract the players by giving a running commentary on what he or she is doing, so that the children are listening to the story and forget to step forward when their ingredient is mentioned.

When that happens, the player is out, or pays a forfeit.

Rearrangement

Divide the players into two teams. The members of the first team are all given names of colours. They arrange themselves in a sequence. The other players are given a minute to memorise the order of the team, and then must turn around and shut their eyes while the first team shuffle their sequence. The players with their eyes shut then open them and have to write down which player was which colour.

Eyes

This game is very simple and pretty silly! But if you have twenty-plus six-year-olds at a party and don't know what to do with them, this should keep them entertained for a while, at least.

You'll need a very large old sheet, or dust sheet, with two small eye-shaped holes cut at the average head-height of the players.

Divide the children into two teams.

Two adults hold up the sheet and one team lines up behind it in single file.

Each player takes it in turns to look out through the eyeholes. The other team has to guess who it is.

Swap over and let the other team have a go at lining up behind the sheet and peering through.

Dick Whittington and His Cat

Two players leave the room and decide on a person and an object associated with that person – like Dick Whittington and his cat, or Tintin and Snowy, or Frodo and the Ring – and which of them is to be which. They then return and are asked questions alternately by the other players in turn until someone guesses correctly both the person and the object. This winner then chooses someone to pair up with as the next person or object and they go out of the room together and decide who and what they are going to be.

This game can easily be reversed so that one or two players are sent from the room while those remaining decide who and what they are going to be. When the players are called back in, one of them has to try to guess the person the players have decided on and the other the object.

Rice Pickers

A good game to play at the party table.

You will need a bag of rice, a saucer and some chopsticks or knitting needles for each player. And a vacuum cleaner for after too, perhaps.

Pour a small number of rice grains into a saucer for each player. Using the chopsticks, each player has to pick up and remove as many rice grains as possible from the saucer in a given time limit.

The player who picks the most grains wins.

Watch out for any cheats who try to simply shove grains from their saucers.

Blindfold Games

Blindfold Feeding

This game can get messy, and young children love it. If possible, it should be played outdoors, but if playing this indoors, it might be a good idea to cover the floor with old newspapers first.

Place two chairs (that you don't much care for!) opposite each other, far enough apart so the children can easily reach each other by leaning forwards. Two children sit opposite each other, both blindfolded. Each is given a bowl of food and a spoon, and must simply feed their partner.

Jelly and ice cream, breakfast cereal or yoghurt are ideal, or you can make it trickier by filling the bowl with chocolate buttons or Maltesers.

The other children at the party can shout instructions if you want it especially noisy. When the bowls are empty another pair can take a turn on the chairs.

(If you are worried about party clothes being spoiled, use some old towels or sheets to tie round the players.)

Blind Man's Bluff

The aim of this game is for the blindfolded player to catch another player, and identify him or her by touch alone.

One player is blindfolded and spun around several times. All the other players scatter and move around, getting as close as they dare to the Blind Man, taunting him or her and tugging at his clothes, and so on, until one is caught.

The Blind Man has to try to identify this person, purely by touch.

If this guess is correct, then that player in turn is blindfolded.

Variation: The players all run about as in Blind Man's Buff, and when one is seized he or she makes an animal sound, barking like a dog, meowing like a cat, or mooing like a cow, for example. The Blind Man has to try to identify the other player by the sound alone.

The Origins of Blind Man's Buff

Blind Man's Buff is for many the traditional parlour game of parlour games. Known originally as Hoodman Blind, when a hood was used instead of a blindfold, the game was common in Britain in the 1500s when it was anything but fun. The person chosen to be It was blindfolded and surrounded by the other players. He was turned around several times to increase disorientation, and then had to try to catch and identify one of the players in the circle. Meanwhile the other players would 'buff' (hit), smack or kick the Blind Man.

Happily, modern versions of the game are much more sedate.

Squeak, Piggy, Squeak

A very funny variation on the Blind Man game, guaranteed to have everyone suppressing giggles. Good for large parties with children.

All players sit in a circle around the Blind Man who stands in the middle holding a cushion, and is twirled around a few times. The Blind Man stumbles about, chooses a lap to sit on and when seated commands, 'Squeak, Piggy, Squeak.' The player whose lap the Blind Man is sitting on has to make a squeaky oinking sound, like a pig. The Blind Man has to guess the Piggy's identity by the sound of their squeaking alone (players should try to disguise their voice as best they can).

If the Blind Man guesses correctly then he or she takes a place in the circle and the Piggy becomes the Blind Man.

Players can be as devious as they like, jumping up to swap places and so on, to confuse the Blind Man as much as possible.

Fox and Geese

The 'fox' is blindfolded, and the 'geese' have to touch him or her without being caught. If one is caught, the goose must stand silently while the fox guesses who it is. If this guess is correct, then the fox changes places with the goose, but if wrong, the game starts again. This can be played until fatigue sets in, or until everyone has been the fox.

Pin the Tail on the Donkey

You'll need a large piece of cardboard or paper; a 'tail' made of pieces of wool tied together, or drawn and cut out on card; some drawing pins and a blindfold.

The aim is to pin the tail on the donkey in the correct place.

Draw a large picture of a donkey (or a monkey, or a horse – anything goes as long as it has a long tail) on the paper.

Pin or stick the picture on a wall – make sure the children can reach it easily.

The first child is blindfolded and spun around a few times, then pointed at the donkey and given the tail to pin to the animal.

Once the tail has been stuck on, remove it, draw a small circle around the pin mark and add the child's initials.

The child whose guess is closest wins.

If you're worried about small children using a drawing pin, you can always substitute sticky tape or Blu-Tack.

Variations: You can draw a large face, and make a large pair of smiling lips in coloured paper for Stick the Smile on the Face, or how about Pin the Mask on Batman?

Eyes-Shut Drawing

The challenge here is for each player to try to draw an object (person, animal, plant) blindfold or with their eyes shut. Pigs are popular choices as are cats – the difficulty and fun are in getting the tail in the right place!

Blind Potato Race

This is a great game to be played in small teams – it can get quite chaotic, with blindfolded players bumping heads in the competitive heat of the race.

Players get down on all fours behind a starting line. They are blindfolded by a referee who then quickly places thirty or so potatoes on the floor around the room.

At the word go, the blindfolded players crawl about trying to collect as many potatoes as possible – stashing them on their person as best they can, under armpits, down a tucked-in jumper, in their trousers or tights – within a minute.

Burglars

A boisterous blindfold game that needs a bit of supervision. It can be played both indoors and outdoors, but the larger the space the better.

Take some chairs, cardboard boxes, baskets, buckets, blankets to wriggle under and so on, out to the garden and make an obstacle course.

All players go through the course a few times without a blindfold, memorising the position of the obstacles as they go.

Then one by one, players are blindfolded, and must negotiate the obstacles as best they can from memory – like burglars creeping around a house at night looking for booty.

Each run can be timed to add a competitive edge. If you have room in the garden, set up several identical courses and turn it into a race.

Smelling competition

Prepare a small number of items which have very distinctive or unusual smells – a lemon, a jar of mustard, a lavender bag, toothpaste, jar of cloves/pepper/salt and other spices. If playing this game with adults or older children, you can vary the items to add a level of difficulty.

Place the items on a tray and cover with a tea towel. Players are blindfolded in turn, and given the items to sniff. They are not allowed to touch or feel them. Each player then goes to a separate part of the room and writes down what he or she thinks the items are.

Variation: If you want to test a different sense, players could guess by taste instead.

Musical Games

Musical Chairs

Musical Chairs is one of a handful of children's party essentials. It's known the world over by various odd names (including, apparently, It's Boring Sitting Like This *in Russia and* Birdie Move Your Nest *in Romania).*

The idea is simple. The game starts with players all seated in chairs which are placed back to back in a line. When the music starts, all must get up and start to walk round the chairs.

As they are walking around the chairs, one chair is removed from the line, so that there's one fewer chair than the number of players. When the music stops all players rush back to the chairs and try to sit down.

The player who fails to secure a seat is out.

Another chair is removed and the game is repeated until there is only one player left.

Variation 1: In a less physically competitive version, there are enough chairs for all the players.

When the music stops, everyone must rush to a seat and lift their feet off the floor as quickly as possible. A referee must decide who raised their legs off the floor last and is then out. Carry on until there is a winner. Pity the referee!

Variation 2: Every player 'owns' a chair to which they must return when the music stops. The last player to get to his or her chair is eliminated.

Musical Statues

As with Musical Chairs, players move around or dance while the music is playing.

When it stops, they must 'freeze' and avoid moving or laughing until the music starts again.

An appointed judge walks among the players and gently tries to induce them to move or laugh. Whoever does so is out and the game continues until only the winner remains.

Musical Bumps

Another great children's party favourite which is especially good for younger children.

The children run about and dance to music. When the music stops, all must sit or drop down on the floor as quickly as possible.

Last one to sit down is out – get ready for the wails of protest!

Pass the Parcel

Another essential children's party game. Be sure to move things on quite quickly and keep the parcel moving to stop active children getting restless and causing havoc.

You'll need one main prize for the last player, and either lots of small prizes such as miniature chocolate bars, or slips of paper each with a joke, riddle or forfeit, to put between the outer layers … and *lots* of wrapping paper or newspapers.

This needs to be prepared in advance – and can be quite time consuming!

A prize is wrapped up in many layers of paper – at least as many layers as there are children. Between each layer of new wrapping paper (if possible, use many different-coloured papers to wrap each layer to make it easier for the children) insert a riddle, or forfeit, or joke written on a small piece of paper, or a sweet or small chocolate bar if you prefer.

The children sit in a circle on the floor and as the music plays, they pass the parcel from child to child round the circle. When the music stops, the child who is holding the parcel may remove one layer of the wrapping paper to reveal the joke, riddle or forfeit, which they then must say out loud, or perform. If you use sweets, they'll know what to do with those!

The child who unwraps the last layer of paper wins the prize inside.

Old School Pass the Parcel

In our day, there was only one prize to be found right at the end when the final layer of paper was torn away.

Now it is normal to create a parcel that has the same number of layers as children attending the party and slipping a small prize – a sweet, or small bar of chocolate, for example – in each layer, timing the breaks in the music so that all children win something. Children will have to learn about disappointment another way!

Party Games Played in a Circle

There are lots of games in which the players are arranged in a circle. This arrangement seems to have been most liked by the Victorians who, frankly, amused themselves in the strangest ways.

Chinese Whispers

A fun game for younger children and great for parties or at the dinner table on any occasion.

It's very straightforward: one player thinks of a word or phrase and whispers it in the ear of the person to the left. That player whispers what he or she has heard (often a very different thing from what was originally whispered) to the next and so on until the word reaches

the person before the originator. This person has to say it out loud
and it is compared to the original word – often with very funny
changes. For example, 'I think you are great' could be mangled into
'I wink at your gate.'

The play then passes to the next person in the circle. It's a good
idea to think of a complicated word or a tongue-twisting phrase that
can easily be misheard when you play this – just to make sure that it
is completely changed by the time it has gone round all the players.
Alternatively, put some loud music on in the background, so it's
really difficult to hear what's being said. Beware of pranksters who
deliberately manipulate what they've heard into something silly.

Turn the Trencher

For this fast-moving game you'll need a wooden plate or something
similar that won't break when spun on its edge.

The players sit in a circle a little distance from the plate which is
positioned in the middle of the circle. Each player is given a place
name. One player starts off by going to the centre of the circle,
spinning the plate on its side and shouting out a place name – the
player who has been given that place name must get to the plate
before it stops spinning and falls over. That player then spins the
object and so on. Anyone who does not make it in time is out. There
are lots of variations as to what the players call themselves – it could
be kitchen utensils, foodstuffs, celebrities or any category in which
there are lots of fun examples.

Tell a Story

The players sit in a circle. One starts telling a story and, when he or
she is ready, points at another player who must immediately continue
the story. When that person decides to pass on the narrator's baton,
he or she points to a different player who must carry on with the
tale and so on, until the last player to contribute points back to the
first player who must successfully conclude the story. No scores in
this one, it's just a nice collaborative game.

Some settings which you might consider for the story: a haunted
house; a desert island; the seaside; the riverbank; outer space.

Farmyard Story

This is a good game for exuberant children.

Every player in the circle takes the name of a farmyard animal – if you run short of names then more than one player can be 'ducks' or 'pigs' or another animal.

One player then tells a story, set on the farm, and every time another player's animal is named, they have to make that animal's noise. If the storyteller mentions the farmyard, then all the players must make their noises together. If a player forgets to make their noise, they are out of the game.

Change

This game requires a little more concentration and skill. You'll need a grown-up to lead the game.

Players sit in a circle and pass round a number of objects of varying weight – as many objects as people in the circle.

On the word 'go' objects are passed to the players' right; on the word 'change' to the left.

If a player drops an object, they are out.

The pace quickens as players, but not items, are eliminated, and it gets more difficult to pass and catch objects at the same time.

The Caterpillar

A very simple game – again a grown-up or someone not in the game can call out instructions.

All players except one sit on chairs in a circle. One stands in the middle of the circle.

The seated players are instructed to move, say, one seat to the left. The standing player must try to sit down on one of the empty chairs as the others move.

The caller can make things more complicated by instructing the players to move three spaces to the left, giving the standing player a much better chance of grabbing a seat.

The person whose seat is taken then takes his or her turn in the middle.

Home!

A more imaginative variation of the Caterpillar, Home! requires the player standing in the middle to tell a story which is made up as he or she goes along.

'I'm going for a walk, it's such a lovely day, the sun is shining,' and so on, any sort of rambling story along those lines.

As soon as the storyteller says the word 'Home' all players have to move to a seat at least three chairs away.

The storyteller tries to grab a seat as quickly as possible.

The person without a seat then stands in the middle and takes up the story.

The Portmanteau Game (or, I Went on Holiday)

This is a memory game best played with at least four players. It requires quite a lot of concentration, so is good for older children of about seven or more.

Players sit in a circle, and the first to go says to the child on his or her left, 'I went on holiday and brought a … ,' naming an item. This child then repeats the sentence, listing the first child's item, and adding another. To make it easier, the objects added can be in alphabetical order, so for example, the first player: 'I went on holiday and brought an anorak.' Player two: 'I went on holiday and brought an anorak and a bathing costume' and so on.

The game continues, with each new child repeating all the previous items in correct order, and adding a new one to the list on each turn, until a player forgets an item or muddles the order of the list. A new round of the game can then be started.

I Went to Town

This is another version of the Portmanteau Game, made slightly trickier by adding actions.

The first player announces to the child to her left, 'I went to town and bought a … ,' naming an item, a banana for example, and then mimes peeling and eating a banana. All the children in the circle copy the action.

The second child repeats the sentence, and adds a new item and accompanying action which the whole circle must copy, along with the first action. So they might say, 'I went to town and bought a banana, and some shoes,' and stand up to mime walking on the spot.

The game continues with each player adding an action. It gets very difficult, very quickly, and if a player misses an item or an action, they are out and leave the circle.

Green-fingered Gardener

One of the children begins the game by saying, 'I am a green-fingered gardener, and in my green-growing garden grows an apple tree.' The next player repeats the sentence, adding another tree or plant: 'I am a green-fingered gardener, and in my green-growing garden grows an apple tree and a rose bush.' The sentence is repeated and added to until players make a slip and are out of the game. The remaining 'gardener' wins a prize. Maybe an apple?

The Elements
A fun and fast-moving game of forfeits.

Players sit in a circle and one player begins the game by throwing a scrunched-up napkin or cloth to another player and calling out one of the four elements – earth, air, fire or water – then counts out loud to ten.

The player to whom the napkin is thrown must shout out the name of an animal that inhabits that element, if it is earth, air or water.

The same animal cannot be named twice and players must call out the animal as quickly as possible – or before the person who threw the ball finishes counting.

If 'fire' is called the player to whom the object is thrown misses a turn and must throw it to another player as quickly as possible – as if it's on fire.

If the player gets the call wrong or fails to respond in the agreed time, she pays a forfeit. (See list on page 27.)

Animal Game
A boisterous memory game which the whole family can play at a big gathering.

The players sit in a circle and whisper the name of an animal to the player to the left. At a signal all make the noise of the animal they have been whispered as loudly as they can for about a minute. All fall silent and players must write down as many as possible of the animal sounds identified and remembered.

Round the Cushion
This is a fairly lively game which might need a referee to blow the whistle if things get too rough.

Six or more players (twelve is more fun) stand in a circle with a good-sized cushion or pillow in the centre.

All hold hands firmly and, on a signal, try to make their neighbours touch the cushion with their feet, pulling them this way and that, while doing whatever is necessary to avoid coming into contact with the pillow themselves.

Once a player has touched the cushion, or let go of a neighbour's hand, he or she is out. Eventually you are left with two people fighting it out to be the winner.

Lonely Ghost

A version of the more grown-up Wink Murder (see page 37), but without the detective, and fun for younger players. You'll need as many playing cards as there are players, one of which is a joker.

Everyone sits in a circle and a dealer gives one card to each player. All players look at their card in secret; the player who is dealt the joker is the ghost.

The ghost tries to turn the other players into ghosts by winking at them as subtly as possible, so that the wink is seen only by the person it's aimed at.

A player who has been turned into a ghost should wait five seconds before saying, 'You got me,' and leaving the circle in ghostly fashion.

If a player catches the lonely ghost winking at someone else, that player wins the game.

Any player who thinks they have guessed who the ghost is can challenge that person, asking, 'Are you the ghost?' If the guess is correct, the ghost must own up; if not, the guesser is out of the game.

The game continues until all the players become ghosts or the original ghost is discovered.

Games to Raise a Smile

Poor Pussy

A good game for very young children, six and under.

Everyone sits on the floor in a circle. One person has to be the 'poor pussy', and crawls around to the other players pretending to be a cat – licking their hands and meowing pathetically.

Every now and again, pussy stops in front of one of the players and looks them right in the eye, pleadingly.

That unfortunate player has to say, 'Poor pussy. Poor pussy. Poor pussy!' without bursting out laughing or smiling. The poor pussy might even attempt to climb into the lap of the chosen player, to make it harder for them to keep a straight face.

Whoever fails to withhold a chuckle, then becomes the poor pussy.

Laughter

The players sit in a circle and the game starts when someone throws a handkerchief – or a similar light object like a balloon – in the air. All the players must immediately laugh out loud, and continue to chortle until the object touches the ground, when they must immediately stop. If any player continues laughing, they must leave the circle and are out of the game. Carry on until there is only one player left, who can perform a victory guffaw if he or she chooses.

Warning: This game can induce hysterics. It's possible that you either won't be able to start laughing, from self-consciousness, or more likely that you won't be able to stop, which can be ruinous.

Throwing the Smile

A great and very simple game for younger children but it's also good as an after-dinner game amongst adults.

Players sit round in a circle. One player is picked to be It.

The chosen person smiles broadly at all of the other players, then wipes the smile off his or her face with the back of a hand and 'throws' it to another player.

That player catches the smile in his or her hand, and places it on his or her lips in turn.

No other player in the circle must laugh or smile; if they do, they are out.

The game continues until there is only one smiling player left in the circle.

The Grand Witch/Wizard

This is a great game for younger children and gives them an opportunity for some elaborate dressing up. It is very simple indeed.

One player, nominated to be the Grand Witch or Wizard, dresses in the most witch-like clothes in the dressing-up box and sits regally on a big chair. The other players gather round, sitting in a circle on the floor, and fawn, pander and make a fuss of her while saying, 'Grand Witch, I adore and worship you, and will serve you in any way you may see fit …' and other such proclamations of devotion and love.

All the time the Witch is pulling the most ridiculous faces she can. As the other players make their proclamations in turn, they have to keep a straight face because anyone who laughs is out of the game. The last person not to laugh is the winner and becomes the next Grand Wizard or Witch.

Active Party Games

Murder in the Dark

One of the classic children's party games.

Tear a large piece of paper into the same number of small pieces as there are players.

Mark one of these pieces with 'X' and another with 'D'. All the other pieces leave blank. Place these papers in a hat (or bowl) and all players step forward to pick one. No one should know who has which piece.

The person who picks the 'D' is the detective. The one with 'X' is the murderer.

All the players congregate in one room – big enough so that everyone can scatter when the lights are turned off.

The Detective switches the lights out. All the others move around as best they can in the dark and the Murderer selects a victim and very quietly whispers, 'You're dead,' in his or her ear.

The victim screams and falls to the floor – leaving enough time for the murderer to move away.

The Detective turns the lights back on, tells everyone to stay exactly where they are and begins to interrogate all the players.

All must tell the truth except for the Murderer who is allowed to lie.

Once the Detective has asked all his or her questions, he or she must accuse someone of being the Murderer.

If the Detective is right, the Murderer must confess; if wrong the person accused has to show why they could not have done it.

This game is even better if you can supply the players with props – a detective's mac or hat, magnifying glass or any other accoutrements that add to the melodrama of the scene.

Post Boxes

A game which should get the children at the party burning off some energy if you're confined to indoors.

Take five shoeboxes (or any other kind of box you can lay your hands on) and cut a big slit in each lid – these are the post boxes.

Next write the name of a country in large letters on the lid.
Distribute the boxes around the room or the house – on the stairs, in
the hallway and so on.

Then prepare a number of small slips (about five times the number
of players) each with the name of either a town or a city in one of
the five countries. There can be several written with the same town
or city. Try to have an equal number of places for each country.

Put all the slips in a single box in the room you're starting the
game from. This box is marked the Sorting Office.

Each player goes in turn to the Sorting Office and takes a slip, puts
his or her name on it and then has to decide on the correct post box
to post the town in and locate it. Players may only collect one slip at
a time, after which they return to get another slip and post that.
Players will take different amounts of time to find the appropriate
pillar box. Then when they come back to the Sorting Office they
have to queue to get the next slip (this alone prepares children for
the adult pastime of eternal queuing in post offices). Once all the
slips have been delivered, the pillar boxes are collected up and the
mail sorted: marks are awarded for getting the slip in the right pillar
box and the player who posted the greatest number correctly is the
winner.

Treasure Hunt

*A good game for all ages – and both outdoors and indoors. It needs quite a lot
of thought and preparation in advance, so best to get ready the night before.*

A treasure, or number of treasures, is hidden in the house or in the
garden, park or wherever you want to play. Written clues, riddles or
a detailed map are used to give directions in order to find the
treasure. The first clue gives instructions on where to find the second
clue, and so on, until the treasure is finally uncovered.

For older children and adults the clues or riddles can be as
complicated as you want to make them, so that a little more
deduction is needed in order to work it out. For instance, 'The first
treasure is in a place where you go to wash your face,' for the
bathroom, and 'Treasure two will surely be found where spices are
kept and smells abound,' for an object hidden in the kitchen. You get
the idea.

For very young children who don't read, you can simply draw
picture clues – the sofa or the bath – to help them find the next clue
and so on.

A couple of things to remember: If there is more than one piece of treasure to seek out always write down where you have hidden them all and make sure the treasure is worth seeking out! There's nothing more disappointing than spending time working out where something is only to find it really wasn't worth the hunt.

Treasure Hunt Bingo

A variation of the Treasure Hunt for smaller children is simply to give each a card with numbers on.

Treasures to be found are each labelled with a number corresponding to one of those on the card, then hidden.

Whoever has found all of the numbered objects first is the winner. It's a kind of Treasure Hunt Bingo.

Home-made Twister

For this game you'll need some A4 pieces of paper, pens and a dice.

Home-made Twister does what it says on the tin.

Write out the numbers one to six on separate A4 pieces of paper – if there are more than four players write them out twice – and scatter the pieces around a room so that the numbers are all within reaching distance (by an arm or a leg) of each other. Next nominate a referee who will roll the dice and adjudicate as the game progresses.

The referee rolls the dice and the first player puts his or her left foot on the number rolled. The referee repeats this for the other players. Once all the players have placed their left foot on a number, the referee rolls again for the first player who this time places his or her right foot on the number rolled. And so on through left hand and right hand. The referee keeps rolling and the players change positions of feet and hands in sequence until someone falls over, at which point they are out.

Last person 'standing' is the winner.

Pass the Waistcoat

This is sort of a grown-up Pass the Parcel … but with dressing up in each round instead of a prize.

Fill a bin-liner or large bag with dressing-up clothes, swimsuits, underwear, gloves, wigs, hats and other absurd pieces of old clothing. The more outlandish the better.

Get everyone dancing to some good dance music. As they dance they pass or throw the bin-liner full of garments from person to person.

When the music stops whoever is holding the bin-liner takes a piece of clothing out; he or she then has to put it on and the game continues.

When the bag is empty, you can judge who is the most absurdly or entertainingly dressed.

Tight Fit

This is a game that needs a bit of preparation. Before the party starts, gather together an assortment of everyday household objects – hairbrushes, fruit, sponges, empty plastic bottles, basically anything unbreakable of that kind of size. You'll also need a pair of tights each for half the number of guests you're expecting.

When you're ready to play the game, divide the guests into pairs and put a pile of objects in front of each pair of players. Put a marker down for a finishing line – it could be the other side of the room or the end of the garden if you're playing outdoors.

On the word 'go' one player of the pair grabs the tights and puts them on. The other player can help before stuffing all of the objects into the tights. Once all the objects are in the tight-wearer has to run to the finish line: first one there is the winner. Simple and great fun.

Team Games

Balloon Race

Divide players up into two teams and give each a balloon.

The players stand in a line behind one another. On the word 'go', each team must pass the balloon up the line of players and back again as quickly as possible, passing it up over heads to the end of the line. When the last player receives the balloon, he or she runs with it to the top of the line, then passes it back once again, this time through his or her legs. The balloon must be passed all the way back to the last player, who then repeats the process, running back with the balloon to the top of the line.

Sometimes the actions are alternated so that one player passes it overhead to the next, who then passes it through his or her legs.

The play continues until all the players have reversed their position and the first player is once again at the top of the line. The first team to do this is the winner.

If the balloon is dropped and touches the floor, that team must start again from the top.

Variation: This game can be played with various different objects – the more awkward the better. One variation is called Pebbles and simply requires the two teams to pass five pebbles (or marbles) one at a time, down the row and back up again.

The first to get all five pebbles back to the starting player is the winner.

Heading Balloons

This is good to play in a larger room. It is a team relay race so divide the players into two (or more) teams of equal numbers of players and have them each stand in a line at one end of the room. Give each team one balloon. On the word 'go' the first players from all the teams set off towards the opposite end of the room, heading the balloons as they go. They have to touch the opposite wall, run back (still heading the balloon) and when they get back to their team-mates head the balloon to the next player for the second player to carry on. This continues until all the players in the team have headed the balloon to and from the opposite wall. First team to get all its players back is the winner.

Balloon Jousting

This is an excellent team game for letting off steam – we play it both in the garden and indoors.

You'll need some string and a rolled-up newspaper and a balloon for each player – one colour per team and one balloon per player (so if you have two teams of five players you'll need five balloons of one colour and five of another).

All players tie their team-colour balloon to their ankle.

At the call of 'joust', all run around trying to whack and pop each other's balloon. The last team with a balloon intact and attached to an ankle is usually exhausted, and the winner.

Pass the Orange

This is a classic party game and a good one for children as well as adults – who may or may not yet know each other very well! Good for breaking the ice.

The players form two equal lines and attempt to pass an orange from one person to the next (and back again), but using only the chin and chest to pass the fruit. (Or by any other means they can contrive as long as no hands are used at any stage.)

If (or rather, when) the orange is dropped, the player who is receiving the orange has to pick it up – again without using any hands.

It might be useful to decide a time limit before you start, should the skill of the players not be up to much.

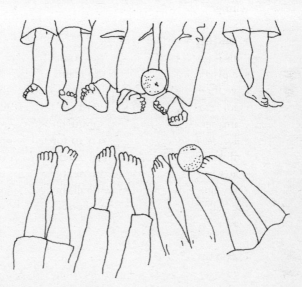

Passing the Orange (feet version)

This is another team race game, but this time the orange is passed using only the feet. Quite a tricky feat.

Players are seated on two rows of chairs facing each other.

An orange is started at one end of the row and must travel to the other end of the row, passed along on top of the players' feet.

The trick is to keep the feet tightly together and the legs stiff, and tilt them to roll the orange gently on to the next player's feet.

The team that gets the orange to the end first, wins.

Teaspoon Race

Players are seated in two rows opposite each other. Each has a plastic teaspoon in their mouth. The first player at the end of each row places a sugar lump in his or her teaspoon, and must pass it along by tipping it carefully into the next player's teaspoon.

The team to successfully get the sugar lump to the end of their line, wins.

Hagoo

This is a team version of a 'stare out' contest.

Players are divided into two teams. They stand in a line facing each other thereby forming a 'tunnel'.

One player from each team stands at the opposite end of the tunnel and slowly walks towards the other, maintaining eye contact.

Neither player must smile or laugh – the players forming the tunnel do their utmost to make the player from the opposing team collapse in giggles or at the very least break into a smile.

Oranges and Lemons

A game for children which can be played either indoors or outside, depending on numbers and on the weather.

Two of the taller children stand opposite each other and form an arch by joining hands high above their heads.

Of the two, they decide who is to be Oranges and who Lemons. Once decided they start to chant the rhyme on the next page and the other children skip through the arch, each holding on to the other's shirt or top.

Oranges and Lemons
Say the bells of St Clement's
You owe me five farthings
Say the bells of St Martin's
When will you pay me
Say the bells of Old Bailey
When I am rich
Say the bells of Shoreditch
When will that be
Say the bells of Stepney
I do not know
Says the great bell of Bow
Here comes a candle to light you to bed
And here comes a chopper to chop off your head

As they chant the last words, the arches lower their arms and catch one of the players.

In a whisper they ask the captured child which side he or she wants to be on – Oranges or Lemons.

The captured child then stands behind the arch on the side they chose.

The game continues until all players have been caught and are standing behind an arch.

When all Oranges and Lemons are lined up behind the two, an adult puts a handkerchief or very short length of rope between the two team leaders and then there is a tug of war to decide which team has won.

Newspaper Race

Players line up at one end of the room. Each is given two sheets of newspaper.

The aim is to race to the other end of the room, by stepping only on the newspaper sheets; they must only have one foot on one sheet at any time, so they have to balance on one leg as they manoeuvre the other sheet of paper forward.

Games to Calm Things Down

Sleeping Lions

This is an excellent game to get everyone to calm down before home time.

Get all the children to lie down on the floor and be as quiet and still as they can. Give them a minute to completely calm down before you (and other adults if you want) slowly move amongst them and gently try to tease them into making a sound or movement. Any child who moves, giggles or fidgets is out. If you want you can get the children who are out to help the adults. Last player left on the floor is the winner.

Statues

Another good party game to play when you want things to calm down for a little while.

One player is the Sculptor. The other players each adopt a pose and must stand absolutely still.

The Sculptor then walks amongst his Statues, stopping to rearrange them in comical postures, moving their arms or legs into odd angles and positions.

They must remain stony-faced and still all the while and the Sculptor can use any means to make the Statues laugh – pulling funny faces, grimacing and so on, but no tickling or touching is allowed.

Anyone who topples over or laughs is out and the last Statue standing becomes the Sculptor.

An Observation Game

A very simple game but it can be good fun with children as they tend to notice things that adult eyes simply pass over. Gather all the players in one room and give them each a pen and paper. Now get them in a minute or two to write down all the things they can find in the room beginning with a specific letter. The kitchen is good for this kind of game.

The Estimators

An odd but quite fun game for slightly older children. It requires the host to do some preparation beforehand, measuring various different objects in a room as well as the room itself, and writing down the dimensions. When the game begins the players are asked, for example:

- ★ height of the room
- ★ length and breadth
- ★ area of a window
- ★ width of curtains (jointly or separately)
- ★ diameter of table

and so on. The other players write down their answers and the winner is the one closest to the most measurements.

Guess the Number

This is another estimating game. One person counts out a number of different items – pins on a pin cushion, buttons in a jar, a length of string, a dish of beans, sultanas on another and so on. Players have to guess how many of each item there are, or the length of the string, and write down their answers.

   Once the correct measurements are revealed, the difference between what each player has estimated and the actual answer is calculated and the player with the lowest score wins.

LIST OF FORFEITS

Forfeits are the icing on the cake of many games. They can, of course, be an evening's entertainment in their own right, but we don't have room for that many in this book. Although they're often meted out as punishment for losing, they're meant as a light-hearted extension to the game, and care should be taken that they never become more than that!

   Many people see forfeits as another chance to show off their singular talents, and good for them. Here's a list of forfeits sorted very roughly into age groups. The severity of the forfeit should really be tailored to the intimacy of the group of players – if you don't know each other that well then start with more neutral or less humiliating stunts; you can always take the kid gloves off later.

Innocent – for Young Children
- ★ Frown for a minute.
- ★ Dance for a minute.
- ★ Repeat the alphabet backwards.
- ★ Do the exact opposite of three things commanded by the other players.
- ★ Crow like a cockerel, moo like a cow and then bark like a dog.

* Say 'gig whip' very quickly six times in succession (or perform any other tongue twister until the other players are satisfied you have got it right – see pages 229–230 for Tongue Twisters).
* Hold your hands together and put them under your feet and over your head.
* Count as far as you can with a single breath.
* Sing the verse of a song.
* Spell your (full) name backwards.
* Talk for one minute about a farmyard animal of your choice.

For Families – Two People of Different Ages
* Put all the pieces into a toddler's shape-sorter toy, taking turns.
* Name three animals which your partner represents through actions and/or sounds.
* Solve a toddler's jigsaw puzzle (about ten pieces) together.
* Recite a nursery rhyme, taking turns with each line.
* Work together to build a tower from wooden blocks, to a time limit of one minute.
* Sing a duet on a karaoke machine.
* Swap and wear one item of clothing.
* Both should stand on one leg while everyone else counts to ten. If one of you fails, you must both start again.

For Grandparents
* Name your first school teacher or the first school you went to.
* Name the first person you fell in love with.
* Give everyone at the party a piece of advice, including the words, 'In my day …' each time.
* Spend ten minutes tied to the person at the party whose birthday is closest to your own.
* Give a one-minute talk on your sporting hero of the twentieth century.
* Make a tower from playing cards.
* Hum your favourite tune and have people guess what it is.

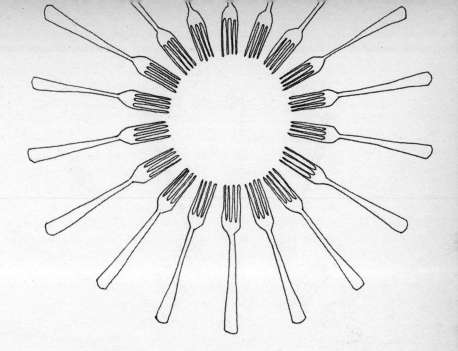

DINNER PARTY GAMES

When you're all sitting round the dinner table, digesting, there are some stimulating games that you can play to get the brain in trim even if you've just piled on five pounds in one sitting. This section has some great games for all the family, and some for adults only.

Games for Mixed Age Groups

Consequences

Consequences is one of the all-time favourite party and Christmas games. We used to play for hours at a time with the 'consequences' becoming more and more absurd as round led to round. It can be adapted according to the age of the group you are playing with and so works just as well as a silly adult after-dinner game as it does with a group of ten-year-olds on a rainy day – summer or winter.

It is a game best played by three or more players, but can be played by just two.

The basic idea is that each player tells a separate part of the same story without knowing what the other players have written. Each player starts with a long strip of blank paper (say about 8cm wide by 20cm long) and everyone writes down their entry for the first part of the story (see below). They then fold the paper over so that their sentence can't be peeked at and pass the folded paper to the player on the left.

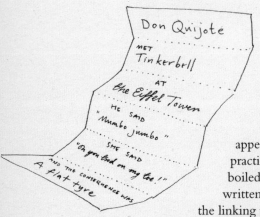

When all the categories have been written, the strips are unfolded and the players in turn each read out the story of Consequences.

A full list of story components appears at the end of this entry but in practice most games of consequences are boiled down to **Entry**, meaning the part written by the players; and **Story**, meaning the linking parts of the story people say as they pass the paper to the next person.

Entry: *The name of a man*
Story: MET
Entry: *The name of a woman*
Story: AT/IN
Entry: *Where they met*
Story: HE SAID
Entry: *What he said*
Story: SHE SAID

Entry: *What she said*
Story: THE CONSEQUENCE WAS
Entry: *The outcome of the story.*

Below is an extended list of the different elements you could
incorporate into your story:

★ one-word description of man
★ his name
★ what he was wearing
★ what he was doing
★ one-word description of woman
★ her name
★ what she was wearing
★ what she was doing
★ person he would rather have met
★ where
★ what he thought
★ what he said
★ what she thought
★ what she said
★ where they went
★ what they did
★ consequence
★ what the world said

Here's an example (italics indicate what players write, CAPITALS is
the story):
Handsome Richard
WEARING
a polar bear costume while walking the dog
MET
supple Britney
WEARING
traditional German dress on her way to Glastonbury
HE WOULD RATHER HAVE MET
Mahatma Gandhi
AT/IN
the launderette
HE THOUGHT
I'm dreading this interview

HE SAID
'I'll have some scrambled eggs please.'
SHE THOUGHT
I really must start saving those coupons.
SHE SAID
'I want to be in your gang.'
STORY PART??? THEY WENT???
They went to Anfield
to do some clay-pigeon shooting
AND THE CONSEQUENCE WAS
They lived on a desert island
THE WORLD SAID
May as well be hung for a sheep as a lamb

Picture Consequences

This game – a variation on the written game Consequences –
actually has a recognised artistic heritage. André Breton, the driving
force behind the Surrealist movement in 1920s Europe, liked to play
this game which he and his circle called Exquisite Corpse. The game
can definitely produce unexpected – and, yes, at times surreal –
pictures.

As in written Consequences, you start with a long strip of plain
paper. The first player starts by drawing a head, folds over the paper,
marks where the neck should begin and hands it to the next, who
then has to draw a segment of the body without seeing what has
been drawn before.

The pictures are revealed once all the agreed body parts – head,
torso, legs, feet and so on – have been drawn.

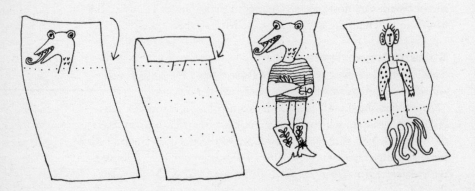

Draw Your Own Conclusions

A great game for four or more people which tests imagination, writing and drawing skills. Great fun when played after dinner.

The first player writes a sentence then passes the paper to his or her right.

The next player draws a picture depicting the sentence as closely as possible, folds the paper so that only the picture is visible, and passes it to the next player, who writes a caption for the picture, then folds the paper over so that only the caption is visible.

Once the paper returns to the first player, he or she unfolds it to reveal the original sentence and the bizarre workings of the players' minds.

The Hat Game

Each player tears a sheet of paper into ten and writes a name on each piece, before folding them in two and putting them into a hat or similar container. They can be the names of celebrities, well-known public figures or fictional characters – as long as the categories are agreed on beforehand.

Now the first player takes a piece of paper from the hat and, after looking at the name, has to describe that character to the person on the left. The description may include what the character looks like, what they do, even an impression of them, but the player mustn't, obviously, say the name. The guessing player can only say names – they are not allowed to ask questions. As soon as the correct name is given, the player describing gives the piece of paper to the guesser and takes another from the hat. They have a minute to get through as many names as possible. Then the guesser takes their turn, describing the characters to the player on their left. The winner is the one with the most pieces of paper in their pile at the end of the round, or when all the names from the hat have been guessed.

Culture Connections

This is a good fast-paced game for later in the evening and probably best played by adults or older teenagers. A good memory is essential.

One player starts off by saying the name of a film, book or play – you can agree on which – and then it is a free-for-all to say the next name which contains one or more of the words in the title. So someone might start with *A Winter's Tale*, which could be followed with *A Tale of Two Cities* and then *Catch-22* and so on. As you play, you'll need to keep a tally of your own points on your fingers. First person to get to ten wins the game.

You can make the game more specialised if everyone round the table shares a particular interest – theatre, film, music or literature, for example. In this variation, one person suggests a word and the game is to come up with as many titles using that word in your agreed category.

Yet another variation is to try to connect song lines by a single word. This does involve some singing which can add to the fun and, remember, the quality of voice matters very little: it's the speed of the connection.

Ghostwriter

This game is one for your inner author. It requires a random selection of books, a pen and some paper.

One player takes the lead for a round and selects a book. He or she shows the book cover, reads the blurb and the author note and gives any other useful bits of information (when it was first published, for example). The other players then write down in secret what they think the first sentence might be. All entries are passed back to the lead player for that round who, in the meantime, has written the actual first sentence down. The leader then, exactly as in Call My Bluff, reads out each entry and the other players take it in turns to say which they think is the real one. (It is worth making the point before you start that all entries should be as legible as possible. If the person reading out the sentences struggles to read your entry, it is clear that it is not his or her own handwriting and therefore not the correct answer!) The points are allocated as follows:

★ One point to a player whose fake opening sentence is chosen
★ Two points to a player who guesses the correct sentence
★ Two points to the round 'leader' if no one picks the correct first sentence
★ Five points to anyone who has written the correct first sentence

The next player then picks a book and you start another round. Play until you've been through all the books or someone has reached an agreed number of points.

It Could be Worse

One player starts the game by making a simple and rather bland statement about something that happened to them, such as, 'I had to go to the dentist yesterday,' or, 'It was raining when I went to the seaside.' The player to their left follows this by thinking of how that situation could have been made even less enjoyable: 'It could have been worse: you could have slipped over on your way.' The next player then must try to build on this: 'It could have been worse, you might have broken your leg and had to crawl to the nearest phone.' The game goes on in this fashion until the statements reach a dead end (!) and the game can then be started again with another innocent scenario. It can be fun, in this game, to try and stretch out the misfortunes rather than going straight towards catastrophe.

Wink Murder

This timeless game, also known as Killer, is brilliantly versatile in that it can be played pretty much anywhere and any time, as long as you have a pack of cards, or at the very least some slips of paper, and at least four players.

The players sit round a dinner table or in a circle. A dealer takes the same number of cards from a pack as the number of players – one of the cards should be the ace of hearts, for the Detective, and another should be the ace of spades, for the Murderer. (If you don't have a pack of cards, make a number of slips of paper and mark one M and another D, leaving the others blank.)

The dealer gives each player one card face down. The player who has received the ace of hearts declares himself or herself as the Detective, all others look at their card secretly. The one who has received ace of spades is the Murderer.

Players now carry on as normal, chatting to each other until the Murderer manages to catch someone's eye and sneakily wink at them. This person has now been killed, and must slump or feign death.

The Detective's role is to try to identify the Murderer as quickly as possible, while the Murderer's aim is to claim as many victims as quickly as possible by winking at them, without being caught in the act by the Detective. The Detective may only make two incorrect guesses as to the Murderer's identity, after which the Murderer wins.

Drinking Games

Should your after-dinner games stretch further into the evening, then a few gentle slurps of something slightly stronger than squash or ginger beer might be welcome. Here is just a very small selection of games for those over eighteen.

High – Low

You'll need a pack of cards and some money – or at least something to bet with.

This was a game played by us on a memorable night in Donegal – snowed in (if you can believe it) in a tiny bar with the peat fire glowing red, a pack of cards and rapidly emptying wallets. It requires no skill but a level of enthusiasm for hazarding a guess and a suicidal attitude to money. It is as simple as it is infuriating.

All the players sit round in a circle and are each dealt one card. Without looking at it, all hold their card on their forehead, displaying it to the others. Players now take it in turns to bet on whether their card is the highest.

So if everyone else's cards are low you might feel brave and put down a high bet, otherwise it's simply a leap in the dark. All players have to bet and after everyone has done so, the cards are revealed and the highest card wins the pot. If there is a tie then the pot is retained for the next round. This is also a good game for deciding who gets the next round in – lowest card goes to the bar!

Cardinal Puff

An intricate game that demands complete concentration and excellent coordination – not skills necessarily to the fore when you've eaten a huge dinner. Cardinal Puff requires you to complete a number of complicated actions in a specified sequence. Each player must take it in turns to perform each round – if they fail they either take a forfeit or drop out of the game or both, depending on how cruel you're all feeling.

The player nominated to start must say, 'I dedicate the first drink of the night to Cardinal Puff,' and then must perform the following actions:

Tap the table top once with the index finger of both hands; tap the underneath of the table once with the index finger of both hands; click the fingers once (again both hands); pick up a glass using finger and thumb; tap the table using the glass, tap the glass in the air with a finger and then take a short drink.

Now everyone else does exactly the same until the turn reaches the nominated player again. He or she starts a new round by declaring, 'I dedicate the second drink of the night to Cardinal Puff Puff.' In this round the same actions as the first round are performed but wherever one finger was used last time he or she uses two and whenever something was done once it is now done twice. So tap the table top twice with two fingers from both hands; tap the glass twice and so on. At this point all the other players will be scrutinising each others' moves very carefully indeed.

The round is played out and the first player starts the final round, this time trebling everything. So he or she declares, 'I dedicate the third drink of the night to Cardinal Puff Puff Puff,' and so on. The leader finishes with a flourish – drinking down in one and putting the glass on his or her head perhaps – and declaring, 'Once a cardinal, always a cardinal.'

You can of course establish your own set of actions and words for this game – whatever suits your family or party best. Some people are so competitive that they nominate a referee before the game starts – a sort of third umpire – who judges whether all the actions have been performed properly and in the right sequence.

Absent Friends

This is a slightly more dynamic version of Cardinal Puff in which the sequence of actions and words is created by the guests one by one as they sit around the table. The first player explains what's about to happen, stands up and proposes a toast. The toast can be to anything – a relative, an event, an invention, a future happening, whatever occurs. She or he then takes a sip of whatever drink is in front of them (and everyone round the table does the same) before performing one simple action – clicking fingers, nodding the head, tapping the person to the left on the shoulder, blowing a raspberry or anything else.

The person to the left then stands up, proposes a different toast, takes a sip, and performs the first player's action before adding a new one. The toast is passed to the next person and so on so that a sequence of actions has to be performed after each unique toast. If you forget the sequence or miss an action then you must either drop out of the game or pay a forfeit.

The last person to complete the entire sequence is the winner.

Ping Pong Beer

This is a game for two teams which requires accuracy, a steady hand and a keen eye. A game, in other words, at which you get progressively worse over the course of the evening. To play it you'll need thirty-two plastic cups, two table-tennis balls, a long table and a plastic covering for the table.

Divide the players into two teams and station one team at each end of the table. Each team builds a pyramid of plastic cups at their end, consisting of ten cups placed in a triangle with six cups on top. As you make the base triangle fill each cup with beer (or the sense-befuddling drink of your choice) and also fill the six cups on top.

The teams take it in turns to try to bounce their ping-pong ball into the cups at the far end of the table. If a player succeeds then a member of the opposing team has to drink the contents of the cup that the ball landed in. Play continues until one team has cleared the cups or you all end up under the table.

Ibble Dibble

This is a very silly drinking game which ends up with players covered in black spots. The format of the game is simple when you're sober, less so when you've had a few. To play it you'll need some corks (real ones, not the plastic kind) and a box of matches or a lighter.

Each person round the table is given a number – so one player is Ibble Dibble One, the next Ibble Dibble Two and so on. Dibble Ibbles are black spots made by marking the face with the burnt end of a cork.

The first player starts the game by announcing his or her name and number of spots (all players are spotless at the start), then passes the play to someone else.

So, for example, 'I, Ibble Dibble One with no Dibble Ibbles call Ibble Dibble Three with no Dibble Ibbles.'

Ibble Dibble Three must then repeat the formula, passing on to Ibble Dibble Seven, for example.

If a player makes a mistake – a hesitation, muddling the wording, or stating the wrong number of dibble ibbles, then he or she is marked with a black cork spot to the face and must drink a shot.

It sounds simple (and silly) enough – but as the evening wears on and drinks keep flowing, it can prove quite challenging as well as hilarious.

The game continues until you've all had enough – in whatever sense 'enough' is enough for the players!

LIST OF FORFEITS

Forfeits at grown-up dinner parties tend to revolve around taking another drink, but here are some more suitable for mixed age groups.

★ Put lipstick on the person next to you.
★ Have a moustache drawn on you.
★ Make two people laugh by telling them jokes.
★ Do an impersonation of John Cleese being Basil Fawlty.
★ Do an impersonation of Alan Rickman as Professor Snape.
★ Say four very complimentary things about yourself.
★ Rub your stomach with your right hand at the same time as patting the top of your head with your left hand. Change to left hand for tummy rubbing and right hand for head patting. Keep this up for one minute. If you forget – start again!
★ Nurse a pillow and sing a lullaby to it.
★ Yawn until you make another player yawn.
★ Eat some dry crackers (without having a drink) then whistle a song, which others have to recognise.
★ Do an impression of a sumo wrestler.
★ Pretend the person on your left is a police officer – now explain why you are wandering along the high street at 3 p.m. in your pyjamas.
★ Get a matchbox and push it along the floor at least three feet, using only your nose.
★ You are truly, madly, passionately in love with the person on your right – go down on one knee and propose – telling them why they should accept your proposal.
★ Answer yes to every question asked by every player in the group.
★ Blow out a candle blindfolded.
★ Swap socks (or another item of clothing) with the person on your left.
★ Suck an ice cube to the end.
★ Be blindfolded and then attempt to put lipstick on all the men at the party.
★ Sit with an ice cube down your T-shirt.
★ Perform the 'Agadoo' dance on the front lawn.
★ Spin around ten times then drink a glass of water.
★ Use a toilet roll to bandage one of your arms.
★ Wearing a blindfold, identify two people by just touching their faces.
★ Lay an egg.

EASTER
Games and Pastimes

And Spring arose on the garden fair,
Like the Spirit of Love felt everywhere;
And each flower and herb on Earth's dark breast
rose from the dreams of its wintry rest.

Percy Bysshe Shelley, *The Sensitive Plant*

Easter is a magical time with its roots springing from pagan and Christian beliefs. According to the seventh-century Christian scholar, the Venerable Bede, the word 'Easter' is derived from 'Eostre', the great Mother Goddess of pagan Europe whose feast day was held around the spring equinox each 21st of March.

Our springtime customs are certainly centred around the ideas of rebirth and fecundity, with the Easter bunny or hare, and the Easter egg, being the most famous symbols of this vibrant time of the year.

In fact, the Christian and pagan origins of Easter are linked in the date of our Easter celebrations, which varies considerably year by year. Easter Sunday is on the first Sunday after the full moon that occurs on or after the spring equinox, unless the full moon falls on a Sunday, in which case Easter is the following Sunday. Got that? In practice this means that Easter can fall any time between 22nd March and 25th April, depending on the lunar cycle.

Easter Eggs

Eggs have been an integral part of the British Easter for many centuries. People decorated hard-boiled eggs with bright patterns, symbolising spring and the rebirth of the land. These eggs were called 'pace eggs', or in some regions 'paste eggs', after the Latin word for Easter – 'Pacha'. They were given away as gifts and also used in games and competitions.

Old traditions involving pace eggs are still maintained in towns and villages, particularly in the north of England. In Cumbria and Durham, for instance, Egg Jarping or Egg Dumping is still played at Easter. Players tap each other's eggs in a hard-boiled form of Conkers, until only the winning egg remains intact.

In Lancashire, egg-rolling contests are held each year, with the egg that travels the furthest distance down a hill without cracking being declared the winner. In other contests it's the number of rolls survived by an egg that determines the winner.

The Hop Egg dance involves prancing in and around eggs laid on the floor while trying to avoid any damage.

Pace Egg plays were and still are performed in villages in Yorkshire and Lancashire at Easter. In the old days, the actors would collect decorated eggs from the crowd, along with anything else they could get as payment, to fill up a basket before they started the drama. Characters like Old Tosspot and Betty Brownbags then take part in a good-natured, if sometimes ribald, performance on the Easter theme of rebirth.

EASTER EGG HUNT

Thankfully, as far as most children are concerned anyway, Easter eggs tend to be made out of chocolate these days, and a good way to heighten the enjoyment of these seasonal treats is to organise an Easter egg hunt.

This can be held indoors or outdoors, or both, depending on the weather and how much space is available. We vividly remember the thrill of being released into the back garden with paper clues as to the whereabouts of carefully hidden mini-eggs. It didn't happen as often as we would have liked, probably because it was raining. Anyway, here are a few ideas for organising a hunt of your own.

You can either simply hide the eggs and let them get on with it, or give clues as to the location of each egg, though this will require a bit more preparation and supervision. Remember to hide eggs in places which won't be out of reach for the smaller members of the hunt.

If you're just going to hide eggs try colour-coding them, so one person is sent to look for eggs wrapped in red paper, one for eggs in blue paper and so on, by distributing bits of coloured foil at the start of the hunt to each participant.

If you want a more organised hunt, you can write clues which create a trail, hopefully not of destruction, through your home and garden. You could provide an initial riddle or question to get them on their way, and then either have a chain of clues leading to an Easter egg bounty, to be shared, or have each clue lead to a chocolate egg wrapped in another clue. It depends how complicated you want it to be!

Either way, make sure that the answers can be guessed by all members of the party to avoid, as far as is humanly possible, tears and tantrums. At the same time, don't make it too easy unless you've got something else lined up. Try to disperse the eggs quite widely so all that adrenalin gets used up.

Good places to hide eggs include inside cupboards, behind shelved books, in flowerbeds, in clothes, under cushions and on people! Bad places include near radiators or other heat sources, under heavy items, near glassware or anywhere that heads can be banged. A and E on Easter Sunday is not where you want to be.

If you are setting clues, decide on the trail first, and then think of appropriate riddles or questions for each egg. You could have rhyming clues like:

With the first egg to find,
We're not being unkind,
It's behind a book,
That contains Captain Hook.
(Answer: Behind a copy of *Peter Pan*.)

The second egg is partly in a cup,
Though not the kind from which you sup,
I think that we've ensured,
That you'll get slightly bored.
(Answer: Cupboard.)

OUTDOOR GAMES

Outdoor games happen everywhere that two or more children come together – in the playground, at the beach, in the garden, by the river bank and in the street. Many of these games are ones that adults can happily join in with on family expeditions.

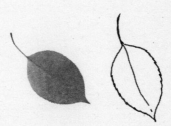

Games, Rhymes and Chants
to Decide Who's It

*Nobody likes to be singled out and the problem with so many games is that
no one wants to be It or to go first. There are as many ways of deciding this
as there are schools or families in the country.*

Children make up the most fantastic rhymes to accompany the
selection of It. The variety is astonishing but what is also intriguing
is how different rhymes are particular to a region. Iona and Peter
Opie made a study of children's games in the 1960s and catalogued
a vast array of different rhymes with as many distinctive regional
variations as there were locations. The rhythms and 'subject matter'
were often the same but the words used were different. The other
remarkable aspect of their research is how long-lived the rhymes are
– many of the rhymes detailed in their book have survived decades
and even centuries and are still in use today in playgrounds across
the country.

Here are some of the many ways of deciding who is to be It
without arguments.

Drawing the Short Straw

Chaucer, in the General Prologue to *The Canterbury
Tales*, suggested that the pilgrims choose lots to decide
who should tell their tale first:

> *Now draweth cut, er that we ferrer twynne;*
> *He which that hath the shorteste shal bigynne.*
> General Prologue, lines 835-6.

This is still a popular method – all you
need is grass, straw, small twigs or even
matches, close to hand. Just make sure
that one is obviously shorter than the rest.
Conceal the end of each straw in your hand but make the ends that
poke out the same length. Have everyone draw the straw and the
player who picks the shortest is It.

Odd Man Out

There are innumerable ways of doing this but the idea is very simple
so it is easy to adapt to whatever circumstances you and the other

players find yourselves in. If you're standing in a group or sitting round a table, the easiest thing is to suggest that, on the count of three, you all perform one of a small number of possible actions. The person who does what no one else does is the loser.

Ip Dip Doo

Players stand in a circle around the person who is the counter and hold out their fists (sometimes feet are counted instead). The person in the middle points at each fist as she or he recites each beat. When the last word of the rhyme is reached, the person whose fist is pointed at removes that fist and only has one life left. The dipping continues until there is only one fist left in at which point that person is declared It. Playground memories abound here – deciding who was to be It sometimes seemed to take up most of break time.

> Ip dip, sky blue
> Who's it?
> Not you.

> Ip dip doo,
> Doggie did a poo,
> Chicken did another one,
> So out goes you.

> Ip dip doo,
> Cat's got the flu,
> Dog's got the chicken pox,
> So out goes you.

In some versions of dipping (say if the players are canny enough to realise who will be counted in) a random element is introduced at the end. When the counter asks the question in the following rhyme, the person pointed at last says a number and the counter then counts round to the person indicated by the number.

> Ippa dippa dation,
> My operation,
> How many people are waiting at the station?

Again there are many variations of this. So sometimes the question requires a colour as an answer and the colour is spelled out with each letter representing a player in the circle.

Eeny, Meeny

Eeny, meeny, miney, mo,
Catch a tigger by the toe,
If he squeals let him go,
Eeny, meeny, miney, mo.
Eeny, meeny, miney, mo,
Sit the baby on the po,
When he's done
Wipe his bum
Tell his mummy what he's done.
Eenie meenie macaraca
Rare raa dominaca
Knikerbocka lollypoppa
Om pom push.

One Potato, Two Potato

One potato
Two potatoes
Three potatoes
Four!

Five potatoes
Six potatoes
Seven potatoes
More!

Ibble Obble

Ibble obble black bobble
Ibble obble out
Turn a dirty dishcloth inside out
Once if it's dirty
Twice if it's clean
Ibble obble black bobble
You are out

Oh Deary Me

Oh deary me
Mother caught a flea,
Put it in the kettle
To make a cup of tea.

The flea jumped out,
And bit mother's snout,
In came Daddy
With his shirt hanging out.

Catching and Chasing Games

Peter and Iona Opie also conducted research into the names that children use for basic catching games. They concluded that the names are regional – so the game is called He in London and the South-East but is predominantly Tig in the North of England and Scotland, Tick in parts of North Wales and the West Midlands and Touch in Devon, Bristol and Hampshire. Some of the less widespread names include Dobby (Nottingham), Stony Picko (Kirkwall, Orkney) and, our favourite, Skibbie (Caithness).

IT GAMES

At their most basic, It games involve one player chasing the others to make one of them It or He by touching them. This is a game most of us will have played at school, and is a perfect way to expend surplus energy during parties or on holidays. Here are some variations.

Glue Tig

In this version of It, whoever is touched must keep a hand on the part of the body where they were touched, while chasing the others. As soon as It has caught someone else, his or her hand is freed. The trick is to try and 'tig' someone in an awkward-to-reach body part, like the foot or back of the knee!

Double It

In this game, two people are chosen to be It. Each time one catches a victim, they have to hold onto them – to become joined together. The joint It then chases other victims, the group It growing in numbers each time. The larger of the two groups at the end of the game is declared the winner. This is a great game to play with lots of players, as each team spreads out in a joined line to entrap escaping players.

Spider and Flies

This is a variation of Double It. Choose someone to be the spider; all the others are the flies.

The spider has to catch the flies by chasing after them. Every fly that is caught by the spider becomes part of its web, and links hands with the spider to catch the remaining flies in the web. It gets easier the more flies there are in the chain. The last player to be caught is the winner, and then becomes the new spider.

Stick in the Mud

This was always a huge favourite. You don't need anything apart from some energy and a playing area. One player is selected to be It. The other players scatter into different parts of the playing area. It tries to tag them. Whenever another player is tagged he or she is 'stuck in the mud' and must stand with legs apart and arms outstretched. It tries to tag as many as possible while the other players try to release those stuck by crawling through their legs. The only time a player is safe is when crawling through someone's legs. The aim of the game is for It to catch all players. You can impose a time limit if you have a lot of players as it can get pretty exhausting; or for a quicker game, once a player has been stuck twice that person also becomes It so there are more and more players trying to do the catching.

Ball Tag

A simple combination of Tag and Dodgeball, the aim of the game is for It to throw a tennis ball (or any other soft ball to hand) to tag other players. The throw should be aimed below the knee. Once you've been hit you're out and the aim is to be the last player in the game.

British Bulldog

Like Red Rover (page 54), British Bulldog has had a bad press. It has been banned in a lot of schools now on Health and Safety grounds but to be honest the level of pain and injury caused by the game depends on which rules you play. When we were growing up it was pretty physical – played in the tarmacked playground with no holds barred. It is perfectly possible, however, to play a tag version of the game which should not involve either hospitals or lawyers.

The aim of the game is to be the last person to be caught. One player is elected as the bulldog and stands halfway between two safe areas; the rest of the players line up widthwise in one safe area. How far apart the safe areas are depends entirely on how much space you've got and how many are playing. If you've got fifteen or more players you'll need about thirty feet separation between the two areas. The bulldog calls out a player who must then try to get to the opposite safe area without being caught. The definition of being caught can range from being wrestled to the ground to being held long enough for the bulldog to say 'British Bulldog one-two-three' to being tagged – you decide on how physical you want the game to be. If the player is caught he or she stays in the middle and becomes another bulldog. If not he is safe.

When the outcome of the first challenge is apparent the rest of the players run across to the opposite safe area and the bulldog tries to catch as many as possible. The game is then repeated from the opposite side until there is only one player remaining. That person is the winner and becomes the bulldog in the next round.

What's the Time, Mr Wolf?

This is a great game for large groups and while it suits larger spaces, like a playground or field, it can be played in a garden too.

One player is chosen to be Mr Wolf. He or she stands at the opposite end of the playing area to the other players, back turned to them. They all chant, 'What's the time, Mr Wolf?' and Mr Wolf answers with the hour ending in 'o'clock'. If Mr Wolf answers, 'Seven o'clock,' for example, the players must take seven steps towards him, counting them out loud ('One, two, three, four …'). Players can decide whether to take bold big steps, or tiny steps in order not to get caught.

The question is repeated, with the players getting closer and closer to Mr Wolf's back, until he or she shouts, 'Dinner time!' and turns to chase them back to their starting position. If Mr Wolf catches one of the players, they then take the place as Mr Wolf for the next round. If, however, one of the players reaches Mr Wolf before the shout of 'Dinner time!' that player is the winner and gets to nominate who is Mr Wolf for the next round.

Witch's Cauldron

This game can be played both indoors and out.

The object of the game is to be the Witch for as many goes as possible.

Players sit on the ground in a wide circle. A large saucepan and wooden spoon are placed in the middle of the circle and a player chosen to be the Witch sits in the middle stirring her 'cauldron'. When she has stirred it a few times, she drops her spoon, rushes to one of the players and touches him or her on the shoulder.

The chosen player and the Witch then must run round the outside of the circle and race each other to the cauldron to grab the stick first. If the chosen child reaches it first, he or she becomes the Witch.

If not, the Witch repeats the game, choosing someone different to race against.

Team Games

Red Rover

This playground game, which can be played in any large outdoor space, is thought to have originated in nineteenth-century England before spreading worldwide as children of emigrants played it in their new lands. It needs quite a lot of players to be enjoyed to its full potential, and with ten or more a side, it is a thrilling game of considerable drama.

The players are divided into two teams called the North Team and the South Team. The teams stand on lines facing each other about thirty feet or more apart. The members of the North Team link

hands, confer among themselves briefly, and then call out, 'Red Rover, Red Rover, we call [name of player from the South Team] over.'

The named player must then run at the other line and try to break through the chain. If the person succeeds in breaking through, then he or she may select either of the two 'links' broken by the successful run, and return to the South Team with them. If the player fails to break the chain, he becomes part of the North Team. The South Team now take their turn at selecting an opponent and calling out, 'Red Rover, Red Rover, we call [name of player from North Team] over.'

The two teams continue to take turns until there is only one player left on one of the sides. If he or she fails to break through the chain, then the opposing team has won.

Capturing the Castle

This is another game which is most fun when played with a large group, preferably more than seven per side. The players are divided into two teams, and the playing area – be it park, field, beach or playground – is divided roughly into two 'countries'.

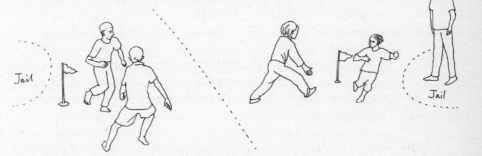

Each team then chooses a base position. This is their 'castle', where they keep their 'flag', which can be any brightly coloured, lightweight object – a T-shirt or towel, for instance. Of course, it can also be a real flag. The most important thing is that it should be easy for all players to spot, and to pick up and carry. The players must also designate another area, at the back of their country, as a jail – where they will keep players captured from the other side. Ideally the jail will be set apart from the castle, but if there are fewer players, it may be better to keep them close together.

Each player must now try to break into the other team's castle and capture the flag to win the game. Whenever a player moves into the opposition's territory, he or she can be caught by being touched or tagged by one of the other team. A player caught in this way is taken to the jail where he or she must remain until one of her team manages to tag her and release her from imprisonment.

It's an exciting game which encourages daring, cunning tactics and initiative. Sometimes it might be better to try to release a player or two from 'jail', and bolster your team numbers, than to attempt to secure the flag in a hazardous dash. Equally, teams will have to decide how many players should stay and defend their territory, and how many should go on the hunt for glory!

Tom Tiddler's Ground

> 'And why Tom Tiddler's ground?' said the Traveller.
> 'Because he scatters halfpence to Tramps and such-like,' returned the Landlord, 'and of course they pick 'em up. And this being done on his own land (which it IS his own land, you observe, and were his family's before him), why it is but regarding the halfpence as gold and silver, and turning the ownership of the property a bit round your finger, and there you have the name of the children's game complete …'
>
> 'Tom Tiddler's Ground', Charles Dickens short story, 1861

The phrase 'Tom Tiddler's ground' referred to the land of someone who was easily taken advantage of although, in this game, that depends entirely on the player who is Tom!

The player chosen to be Tom Tiddler stands or sits inside a playing area designated as 'Tom Tiddler's Ground'. He or she pretends to be sleeping. The other players venture onto this ground chanting, 'Here we are on Tom Tiddler's ground, picking up gold and silver.' They must keep chanting and moving closer, perhaps pretending to pick coins off the floor, until Tom suddenly 'awakes' and runs after them. Tom is not allowed to cross the boundary, but if he manages to catch a player on his ground, then they take over as Tom Tiddler.

Old Stone

This is a variation on Tom Tiddler, with one player crouching down pretending to be a stone. The players get nearer and nearer until the Old Stone springs into life and chases them. In this game there are no safe boundaries and so it continues until a player is caught and becomes the new Old Stone.

Ball Games

French Cricket

No one is sure how the name originated, but one theory is that, just as a so-called 'French cut' is a bad stroke by a batsman, 'French cricket' is a slight at the French, as it is like a poor man's cricket. Ironic given that increasingly simplified versions of the game seem to be getting more popular than three- or five-day matches. This is a great game to play after a picnic, as it doesn't demand too much running around!

You will need a cricket bat or tennis racket and a tennis ball, or any soft rubber ball.

One player is chosen to bat first. He or she stands with feet together, surrounded in a wide circle a few metres away by the remaining players, who are both bowlers and fielders.

In French cricket, the 'stumps' are the batsman's legs below the knee – and the bowlers bowl underarm to (or rather at) the batsman, aiming to hit his or her legs.

The batsman must try to defend his legs and hit the ball away.

If he does, he can move his feet to face in the direction the ball has landed. The fielder/bowler runs to stop the ball or fetch it from its landing place, and then must bowl the next ball from that point.

If the batsman fails to hit the ball, then he is not allowed to move his legs at all, and must stand in the same direction, twisting his body and bat to defend his 'stumps' as best he can.

The batsman can also be 'caught out' if his ball is caught by one of the fielders before it bounces.

When the batsman is either bowled or caught out, he is replaced as batsman by the player who got him out.

Variation 1: Once he has struck the ball, the batsman can only move the position of his feet until the fielder picks up the ball. If he moves after the ball has been picked up, he is replaced by the bowler of the last ball.

Variation 2: The batsman must remain in the same position throughout his innings, and is declared out if his feet move.

Variation 3: The batsman can score runs by passing the bat or racket from hand to hand around himself. Each complete rotation counts as one run, which the batsman must call out – 'One, two, three,' etc. The counting must stop as soon as the ball is in the hands of a fielder and they shout, 'Stop.' In addition, the players may agree a prearranged boundary which, if crossed by the ball without bouncing, counts as six runs, or four runs if the ball touches the ground first, just as in proper cricket.

Hit the Bucket
This game, similar to French Cricket, can be played with three or more players – a batsman and a minimum of two bowlers. Five or six bowlers make it even more enjoyable. You'll need a bucket, a tennis or rubber ball and a bat or racket (improvise with a flat piece of wood if no bat is available).

The batsman stands on top of a bucket and defends it with the bat.

The bowlers take up positions in a circle at a distance of two metres or more from the batsman. The first bowler throws the ball and tries to strike the bucket. The batsman must use the bat to defend the bucket while standing steady on top of the bucket. If he or she strikes the ball, a bowler must run to stop it, and then attempt to hit the bucket from that point. The batsman is 'out' when a bowler strikes the bucket with the ball, catches the ball from a batsman's strike or causes the batsman to overbalance and fall off. The bowler then takes his or her place.

A Ball Race

Players stand in a line and each one has a bouncing ball – ideally a football or basketball, though tennis balls or small, rubber balls could be used to make it more difficult. When the signal to start is given, the players must walk forward bouncing the ball with one hand only, or two hands if agreed beforehand, calling out each successful bounce – 'One, two, three,' etc. If the ball bounces twice, then that player is out for that go. The one who bounces the ball the most times is, of course, the winner.

Sevens

We used to play this for hours against the side of the house. You only need a wall and a tennis ball. The idea is that you perform one action seven times, the next six times and so on down to (the most difficult action) once; and then build back up to the first action again. If you fail one of the actions, the next player has a go until he or she misses or drops the ball and so on. Great for practising accurate throwing and catching. Some actions to try:

★ Throw the ball against the wall and catch (seven times)
★ Throw the ball against the wall, let it bounce once and catch (six times)
★ Throw the ball so that it hits the ground, then the wall and then catch (five times)
★ Throw the ball under your leg, against the wall and catch (four times)
★ Throw the ball against the wall, clap twice and catch (three times)
★ One arm behind the back, throw the ball against the wall and catch (two times)
★ Throw the ball against the wall, turn full circle, clap and catch (once)

The first one to complete the sequence down and back up again is the winner.

Monday, Tuesday

This is a variant on an old Victorian ball game. The aim of the game is for the players, working as one team, to bounce and catch a ball thrown against the wall in the longest sequence without letting it drop to the ground. Ideally this should be played with seven, but it can be played with fewer.

All you'll need is a tennis ball or rubber ball of similar size.

Each player is named after a day of the week. The players group together and decide which 'day' will go first. Whoever this is must shout out the name of a day, other than their own, while throwing the ball against the wall. If the shout was for 'Wednesday', then Wednesday must catch the ball before it bounces on the ground, and then call out another day as she or he, in turn, throws the ball at the wall.

Since the aim of the game is to build up a long sequence of catches, players should try and throw the ball so it is easy for the next player to get to. This is difficult when they also have to decide on a name to call out at the same time.

There's fun to be had in seeing if you can build a sequence of days of the week, starting with Monday and finishing with Sunday.

Blindfold Games

Natural Mystery (Guess Me!)

This is a great game to play on a picnic or at the beach, but it can be played anywhere there's a ready supply of natural objects. If you're playing at the beach, you can use pebbles, shells and seaweed. In the country, flowers, leaves and seeds will do, or maybe items from the picnic hamper. One player is blindfolded, and the other players collect five objects for him or her to feel and smell. A point is awarded for each correct answer. The other players then take their turn to be blindfolded and the winner is the one with the most correct guesses. If two players have the same number of points, then there is a play-off, with the same mystery object being given to both players who must whisper their answer to one of the other participants.

Jingling

This is an old sport, reputedly with its origins in the West Country. Ideally it should be played out of doors, in a defined area, but if it's raining you might get away with using a large room. Just make sure all breakables are out of harm's way.

One player, the Jingler, has a bell or some device that makes a noise, attached to his or her wrist or item of clothing. All other players are blindfolded and must try to catch the Jingler by following the noise as he or she runs about dodging the blindfolded players, taunting and teasing them. Obviously the Jingler will have to decide when to stand totally still and silent, and when to move, thus alerting the others to his whereabouts and risking being caught.

A time limit should be set depending on the size of the playing area. If playing outdoors in a large space, maybe five minutes, if in a large room, a minute will probably be fairer. If the Jingler remains uncaught after this time period, he or she is the winner. Any player who catches the Jingler wins and should become the next Jingler.

Blindfold Race

Another outdoor game best played in a large open space, in a park or at the beach. All players agree a finishing line. The blindfolded players are lined up and paired each with a non-blindfolded player who acts as guide to prevent mishaps. The blindfolded players take their guides by the hand and lead them to where they think the finish line is. The guides may not help them or try to direct them, but must go exactly where they are led.

This game can be made more difficult by adding some soft obstacles along the course.

Walk, My Lady, Walk!

Another great outdoor party activity. This is a variation on an old Victorian game for a large group of children to play in a garden or at the park. You will need a different-coloured handkerchief for each player – a piece of cloth will do just as well – and a blindfold.

Decide who is going to be My Lady and blindfold him or her. All the other players should scatter widely, and drop their handkerchiefs on the ground.

The group then call out, 'Walk, my lady, walk!' and the blindfolded My Lady must set off into the garden. The other players may keep calling 'Walk, my lady, walk!' to encourage him or her in a direction away from their own handkerchief. When My Lady treads on one of the handkerchiefs, the owner is out of the game. She should continue until only the winning handkerchief is left. The winner then becomes My Lady.

Human Croquet

This is a game for large groups of friends, at least eight but parties of twenty or more players work well – and it is ideal for playing outdoors with lots of space, in a big garden, at the park or in a field.

Players should team up into pairs. They will either be playing croquet or forming the hoops – there's no equipment in this version of the game except human bodies. At a minimum you will need two pairs to play croquet and the rest to be hoops.

The pairs who will be hoops spread out over the playing area and form the hoops by standing opposite each other, holding their arms in the air and clasping hands. Each hoop is given a number from one to however many hoops there are – the croquet players must negotiate the hoops in correct number order.

Each of the other pairs comprises a human croquet ball who is blindfolded and the human mallet. The mallet then points the ball in the direction of the first hoop and says, 'go'. The ball moves forward in the direction the mallet has pointed him until the mallet says, 'stop' – either because the ball has gone through the first hoop or has missed. If the hoop has been successfully negotiated the mallet can point the ball in the direction of the second hoop. If not then the second team has a go. If one ball hits another, the striking ball gets another go while the one that has been hit misses a turn. The winning team is the one that has successfully completed the course. Once a game is completed, you can all swap around.

Croquet, despite its probable French origins, is seen as a quintessentially English game. In fact, it only came in its current form to Britain from Ireland in the mid-nineteenth century. Lewis Carroll created the indelible image of the Queen of Hearts at play, using flamingos as mallets and curled-up hedgehogs as balls, merrily lopping off heads as she progresses.

Skipping

Skipping games are as old as rope, and the rhymes that accompany many of them have been passed down over the centuries from child to child, and region to region. Skipping used to be a popular pastime with boys, but sadly they seem to have lost interest, and it has been largely left to girls to keep alive the weird and wonderful poetry of the rope.

Many games are thought to have been introduced to Britain by American families stationed here in the forties and fifties. Many rhymes mutate and develop to assimilate contemporary language, becoming a beguiling, often nonsensical mix of the ancient and modern.

Although it's an activity associated with children and the playground, skipping is a great way to get, and stay, fit and it is used as a warm-up routine by many top athletes.

Just about all skipping games are for three or more players – two to hold the rope (known as 'enders') and at least one to skip. Many of these games have local variations and so it is remarkable how, given that the rhymes can vary so much from town to town, the basic format of the games is consistent and has remained so for generations.

Beci Dale from the UK set a new Guinness World Record in one-minute speed on 24th May 2009 with a score of 332 (166 right-foot skips).

SKIPPING RHYMES

Here are some traditional rhymes or songs which are chanted to accompany skipping games involving three or more children. The rhymes usually have various physical actions which the skipper must perform in time with the chant.

Two enders hold the rope and swing it, while a third or more run in and jump the rope, performing actions in time with the chants. If they stumble or stop the rope, then they swap with the ender who has a go at skipping. In a lot of the games, as the skipper stays in longer, so the enders will turn the rope faster and faster making it harder for the skipper.

For these traditional skipping games you need a long, fairly sturdy rope which will turn well – either a 4.4 m rope for three skippers, or a 7.5 m rope for more than three skippers.

Inky Pinky Ponkey

Inky pinky ponkey
Daddy bought a donkey
Donkey died
Daddy cried
Inky pinky ponkey

Cowboy Jo

Cowboy Jo
From Mexico
Hands up
Stick 'em up [hands in the air]
Drop your guns
Pick 'em up
O-U-T spells OUT

Bubble Car, Bubble Car

Bubble car, bubble car
Number 48
Turning round the co......rner [draw out saying 'corner' as the skipper leaves the rope to run round one of the turners, and then back into the rope]
and then put on the brake [stop the rope between your legs]

I Am a Girl Guide Dressed in Blue

I am a girl guide dressed in blue,
These are the actions I can do,
Stand 'at ease',
Bend your knees,
Salute to the officer,
Bow to the Queen,
Turn your back on the leader of the pack,
And run right through.

Teddy Bear, Teddy Bear, Turn Around

Teddy bear, teddy bear, turn around
Teddy bear, teddy bear, touch the ground
Teddy bear, teddy bear, show your shoe
Teddy bear, teddy bear, that will do
Teddy bear, teddy bear, go upstairs

Teddy bear, teddy bear, say your prayers
Teddy bear, teddy bear, turn out the light
Teddy bear, teddy bear, say goodnight.

SKIPPING GAMES

Copy the Fox
The skippers line up in front of the rope. The two enders start to swing the rope and the first skipper then chooses a step – this could be a star jump or skip on one foot – and enters the rope. When they have exited the rope, the other skippers must jump in, copy the move and then exit.

Next the second skipper enters the rope and does two moves linked together. The other skippers must then try and copy this routine. Then the third skipper puts together three moves, and so on.

Up and Down
This is a difficult skill for the two enders to master, but it's worth it. Using a long rope (7.5 m), one ender starts to turn their end of the rope. When it is at its highest point, the other ender starts to turn his or her end, which results in one end being on the ground while the other is propelled upwards. Two skippers enter the rope at opposite ends, each trying to touch the ground when their half of the rope is over their head, in the air.

The Clock
As they turn the rope, the enders shout out the hours of the day, each of which has an action to be performed by the skipper:

One o'clock [enter, jump once, exit rope]
Two o'clock [enter, jump twice, exit]
Three o'clock [jump three times]
Four o'clock [jump four times]
Five o'clock [jump five times]
Six o'clock [high waters]
Seven o'clock [low waters]
Eight o'clock [hop eight times]
Nine o'clock [hop nine times with one eye closed – single bounce]
Ten o'clock [jump ten times with both eyes closed – single bounce]

Eleven o'clock [jump eleven times with feet crossed one way]
Twelve o'clock [jump twelve times with alternating crossed feet]

'Low waters' is where the rope is held taut just above the ground, and the skipper has to jump over it.

'High waters' is the same, with the rope being held higher – though not at an impossible height.

Lemon Tart

The two enders turn the rope while a skipper jumps over it, all singing, 'Rosy apples, lemon tart, tell me the name of your sweetheart.' Then they shout out the letters of the alphabet. When the player jumping over trips on a letter, they have to think of a person whose name begins with that letter and that is the skipper's 'sweetheart'.

Cinderella

Two enders turn the rope and one person skips, while the enders chant:

Cinderella dressed in yella
Went upstairs to kiss a fella.
By mistake,
She kissed a snake,
How many doctors did it take?
1, 2, 3, 4, ...

The skipper continues to skip until she trips or misses a jump.

All in Together

Two enders turn the rope, with unlimited skippers. The chant goes:

All in together, boys and girls [everyone runs into the rope and starts skipping]
Never mind the weather, boys and girls
When I count twenty, the rope must be empty
Five, ten, fifteen, twenty [everyone runs out of the rope]
When I count ten, the rope must be full again
Five, ten [everyone runs back in]
When I count two, you must touch your shoe
One, two

When I count four, you must touch the floor
Two, four
When I count six, you must do the splits
Two, four, six [jump in the air with legs apart].

Back to Back

This needs two enders and two skippers, using a 4.4 m rope.

Two people stand inside the skipping rope. As the enders start to turn the rope, the skippers start in the centre of the rope, back to back whilst jumping and singing. They then turn to face each other and shake hands and change places at the same time. There are various chants; here is one of the most popular:

Back to back,
Face to face,
Shake your partner's hand and change your place.

If the skippers don't complete the rhyme then they swap places and become the enders.

Alphabet Skipping

The enders swing the rope with an even rhythm. Each child takes it in turn to jump in and skip whilst chanting the alphabet. If they reach Z they jump out. A variation is to chant, 'When it's your birthday please jump in.' The enders chant the names of the months until the first skipper's birth month is announced, and the enders then count through the days. The skipper has to stay in until her day and month have been chanted. If the skipper manages to do that she becomes an ender.

Name Skipping

The enders turn the rope. Each child takes it in turn to jump in, spell his or her own name and then jump out.

Clapping Games

Clapping games are another one of those activities which children enjoy and at which they excel. The blend of physical dexterity, memory and unselfconsciousness that the games demand is possessed in abundance by most young kids and diminished in adults. Having said that, many ex-children have surprised us with their enthusiasm for and recall of these simple games – lots of which have developed their own local, let alone regional, variants – far too many to list here. We've stuck to the tried and trusted.

The beauty of these games is, of course, that the words hardly matter, and there is plenty of scope for the imagination to run riot.

Most clapping games are between two people and involve the chanting of a rhyme or song to developed patterns of claps and hand movements. Some games are competitive but many demand cooperation and help develop social skills. Very often one child will lead with a clapping pattern they have invented, or they will try a new one out on the spot, which the other, or others, will attempt to follow.

These patterns may include clapping your own hands, a hand or the hands of your partner, slapping other parts of the body or touching some object and striking a pose to complete the game.

Double Double

To start with, here's a game in which you don't actually clap, but gets you used to the rhythms involved. Try playing opposite a friend. Your hands should be in the air, pointing upwards. When you're reciting the rhyme, your palms should be facing towards you whenever you say 'double', and away from you, towards your partner, whenever you say 'this' or 'that' (or 'ice' and 'cream' in the variation).

Double double this this,
Double double that that,
Double this, double that,
Double double this that.

Variation

Double double ice ice,
Double double cream cream.
Double ice, double cream,
Double double ice cream.

Simple Clapping Game

Stand or sit opposite your partner. Clap both hands with your partner, palms out. On the beat just clap the right hands together, then both hands again, then just left hands together. Now start adding in your own variations. Clap shoulders, thighs or objects as well, increasing the rhythm and the speed as you get more practised.

CLAPPING RHYMES

A Sailor Went to Sea

A sailor went to sea, sea, sea,
To see what he could see, see, see,
But all that he could see, see, see,
Was the bottom of the deep blue sea, sea, sea.

Suggested actions

A – clap own hands
Sai- – clap right hands with partner
-lor – clap own hands
went – clap left hand with partner
to – clap own hands
sea, sea, sea – clap partner's hands three times
Repeat through the song.

Here are some other well-known rhymes to experiment with and enjoy:

Oh, Jolly Playmate

Oh, jolly playmate! Come out and play with me.
Come, bring your dollies three, climb up my apple tree!
Slide down my rain barrel and through my cellar door.
And we'll be jolly friends for ever more, more, more.

Poor jolly playmate! I cannot play with you.
My dolly has the flu — boo-hoo, hoo, hoo!
I have no rain barrel, and no cellar door,
But we'll be jolly friends forever more, more, more.

Under the Bram Bush

Under the bram bush,
Under the sea, boom, boom, boom
True love for ever,
True love for me.
When we get married,
We'll have a family,
A boy for you, a girl for me,
Um tiddley um dum, cha-cha!

Long-legged Sailor

Make up your own clapping actions with a partner, but each time
you chant 'long', spread your arms wide; each time you chant 'short',
bring your hands together in front of you; and each time you say
'bow', make a loop over your head.

Have you ever, ever, ever in your long-legged life
Seen a long-legged sailor and his long-legged wife?
No, I've never, never, never in my long-legged life
Seen a long-legged sailor and his long-legged wife.

Have you ever, ever, ever in your short-legged life
Seen a short-legged sailor with his short-legged wife?
No, I've never, ever, ever in my short-legged life
Seen a short-legged sailor with his short-legged wife.

Have you ever, ever, ever in your bow-legged life
Seen a bow-legged sailor with his bow-legged wife?
No, I've never, ever, ever in my bow-legged life
Seen a bow-legged sailor with his bow-legged wife.

Have you ever, ever, ever in your long-legged life
Seen a short-legged sailor with his bow-legged wife?
No, I've never, ever, ever in my long-legged life
Seen a short-legged sailor with his bow-legged wife.

Miss Lucy Had a Baby

Miss Lucy had a baby,
She named him Tiny Tim
She put him in the bathtub
To see if he could swim.

He drank up all the water,
He ate up all the soap,
He tried to eat the bathtub,
But it wouldn't go down his throat.

Miss Lucy called the doctor,
Miss Lucy called the nurse,
Miss Lucy called the lady
With the snakeskin purse.

Tarzan

One player alternates clapping their hands and slapping their knees, while the other player does the same, but knees first!

Tarzan jungle man swinging from a rubber band
Fell down, broke his crown
What colour was his blood?

When you get to 'blood', whoever has their hands on their knees decides on a colour. The two of you spell out a colour (for example, B-L-U-E), and whoever has their hands on their knees at the end of the word, must put one hand behind their back for the next go, for which they must nod their head instead of clapping hands. Continue until one player has both hands behind their back, leaving the other player as the winner.

Word Chase

This is a competitive clapping and rhyming game for slightly older children, and is good for developing the ability to think quickly! Players stand in a circle and begin by setting up a rhythm of clapping their own thighs once, followed by clapping their hands together. Once they have counted off aloud four thigh slaps ('One, two, three, four) the first player says a word on the next thigh slap. The player to the right must supply the next word on the next thigh slap and so on, clapping hands on the second beat, until a sentence is formed, at which point the next player can say 'stop' on the next thigh slap. If a player misses their turn, or comes up with a word which they can't finish a sentence to, then they are out and must leave the circle. The last player in is the winner.

Games for a Hot Summer's Day

We all need to cool off when we're outdoors enjoying the summer sun. Here are some refreshing games when the sun's beating down and you can't bear to go back indoors or into the shade.

Water Roulette
You'll need water balloons – filled with water and tied with a knot. Nominate one player to be It. The other players stand in a circle around him or her and everyone (including It) is allocated a number.

The player in the middle grabs one of the water balloons, throws it in the air and simultaneously shouts a number. The person whose number is called has to try and catch the balloon before it crashes and bursts on the ground. If she succeeds, she stands in the middle, picks up a balloon and shouts a number before returning to the circle. If she doesn't succeed, she should leave the game but, before she goes, she picks a balloon, throws it in the air and shouts a number to allow the game to continue.

Last person left in is the winner.

Variation: This game can also be played with a normal beach ball or football instead of a water bomb.

Ballooning Backs
You'll need water balloons for this one too, a companion game to Water Roulette. The aim of the game is for pairs each to wriggle a balloon between their backs in order to get it safely to the ground first.

The players divide into pairs. Depending on how many there are of you, try to team taller players with smaller ones in order to get as much height disparity in each pair as possible: this makes this game much more entertaining. Each pair stands back to back with the water balloon resting between their shoulder blades. At the word 'go', pairs should wriggle and manoeuvre the ball between their backs until it reaches the ground.

If players drop their water balloon without it bursting, they may start again from the top. If their balloon bursts, they are out – and wet to boot.

Arctic T-shirt Competition

You've heard of the wet T-shirt competitions made famous on 18–30s holidays? Well, here's a fun family version, ideal for a steaming hot summer's day. All it requires is a small amount of preparation the night before.

Gather together as many T-shirts as there are competitors.

Soak the T-shirts (one for each competitor) in water and either scrunch them up or fold them and put them in the freezer the day before the competition. When you are ready to play the game, take them out and place one in front of each competitor. The frozen T-shirts stiff with ice are incredibly hard to pull apart and put on and, not surprisingly, freezing cold once they are on. The first person to get his or her T-shirt on is the winner. Or perhaps the loser.

Water Fight at the Blindfold Corral

This is a team game requiring excellent communication skills and fast reactions. Two water pistols, a large bucket of water and two blindfolds are all the props you'll need.

Nominate someone who doesn't want to get soaked to be the town sheriff for the duration of the game. Divide the players into two teams of equal numbers, facing each other in semicircles. In the middle, place two filled water pistols in the bucket of water. Each side's players are assigned a number – one, two, three and so on.

The sheriff calls out a number and the two players with that number step forward to be blindfolded by him or her and then return to their side.

The sheriff then shouts, 'Go!' and the blindfolded players, directed by their teammates' shouts, must locate the bucket, pick up a water pistol and land a direct hit on their opponent. The first player to shoot accurately claims a life for his team. The first team to wipe out the opposing team wins. Everyone should get wet!

Sleeping Bag Showdown

Towards the end of the day – when it's a bit cooler – have a go at this game, which is a must for all sleepover parties or camping trips. It's pretty simple: arm yourself with your pillow, zip yourself into your sleeping bag and come out swinging. Last player standing is the winner. Ideal for letting people get rid of any excess energy before bedtime.

GINGER BEER

'I must say ginger beer is a gorgeous drink – it seems to go with everything.'

Julian, *Five Run Away Together*

No other drink quite conjures up the short-trousered version of pre-television childhood – whole summers spent playing in fields before returning for sandwiches, cake and, of course, ginger beer. It is a simple symbol of carefree days.

Ginger beer was first brewed (in the mid-eighteenth century) as a small beer – a weakly fermented concoction which was drunk as an alternative to the bacteria-laden water of the time. The refreshing zing as well as the known health-giving benefits of ginger made it an increasingly popular 'soft' drink. In the early nineteenth century it was sold from stalls and mobile soda fountains. Some vendors made their own to sell while others rented a concession to do so, and it was often the trade of those who had talent for little else. There are accounts of Victorian gentlemen gratefully stopping at a ginger beer stand to help cure their hangovers on Sunday mornings before a day out with the family on Hackney Marshes. It could also be brewed to strength to rival the strongest beers of the time – a situation that horrified temperance campaigners until, in 1855, the British Excise Regulation established that ginger beer should contain no more than 2 per cent alcohol. Now it is only really available in big plastic bottles or tin cans as an alcohol-free soft drink (though an enterprising Scottish firm produces an alcoholic version) and the tradition of brewing ginger beer at home is largely a thing of the past.

Lost, too, somewhere in local folklore is the origin of the staple of so many school summer fairs: the ginger beer plant. It is a curiosity of ginger beer that it can be made from scratch using 'normal' ingredients (ginger, sugar and water) but it can also be produced by garnering and cultivating a 'plant'. The plant is not a naturally occurring substance and, to this day, no one knows where and how the first one was made. Its ingredients, however, were established in 1887 by Henry Marshall Ward who became obsessed with finding out the active components of the plant. Five arduous years later, he established that the plant was a living organism rather like lichen. Ward managed to create a plant of his own which is rumoured to have survived to the 1940s. The plants, once 'alive', needed to be fed with sugar to keep them going and also could be separated into smaller plants and passed on to other people. This of course made ginger beer extremely cheap to produce – once you had a plant you only needed sugar and water and a vessel to brew the beer in. The plant was handed down through the generations until, it is thought, rationing of sugar during and after the Second World War made it more difficult to keep the plants alive. Since then the trade in plants has nearly dried up – but there are a few places where you can still order them.

Ginger beer can be made in a variety of ways and can of course be either alcoholic or soft depending on your taste. If you want to make an alcoholic ginger beer, simply follow the recipe below and allow the fermentation process to continue beyond five days. One overall health warning though: never use glass bottles as the pressure from the fermentation can easily cause explosions. There are a few internet sites to look up if you want to order, or even grow, your own living ginger beer plant and make the ginger beer from that.

Basic Ginger Beer Recipe
This is a really basic recipe – it only takes a few minutes to make and will be ready in twelve to thirty-six hours. It makes 2.5 litres.

Ingredients
1 tablespoon finely chopped ginger
1 unwaxed lemon (thinly sliced)
250g caster sugar (golden is best)
½ tsp cream of tartar
¾ tsp fast-action yeast
2.5 l bottled water (tap is OK but bottled tastes better)
2 x 1.5 l empty plastic bottles with screw tops. (Wash with soapy water, rinse thoroughly and then sterilise using a liquid sterilising solution. Rinse again and allow to dry.)

Put 750ml cold water (the purer the water the better the taste) into a large saucepan and add the ginger, lemon slices, sugar and cream of tartar. Gently bring the water to the boil while stirring continuously to help dissolve the sugar. Simmer for five minutes, then add the remaining water and sprinkle the yeast over it. Put the lid on the pan and allow to cool overnight.

In the morning pass the ginger beer through an ordinary nylon sieve and put it into the two plastic bottles. Remember to leave a gap at the top of the bottle (about an inch and a half) to prevent too much of a build-up of pressure – you should also look to release a little gas every few hours by unscrewing the cap a fraction and then tightening it again.

The ginger beer is ready to drink when it's fizzy (start checking about twelve hours after you've bottled it).

Beach Games

Splash by Numbers

You'll need to take some card or paper with you, cut into numbered squares, one for each player. You'll also need a bag or hat to draw the paper squares from and a container for water – say a plastic bottle, a sand bucket or a beaker.

This is a great game for the beach on a hot summer's day, should one occur, though it can also be played in the garden. All participants should be warned that they are going to get WET, and therefore to wear something that will dry quickly, or which can be replaced with little inconvenience!

If eight players are taking part, you will have eight small cards with the numbers one to eight. Put the numbered cards into a hat or bag. One player starts by picking a number out of the bag, shows it only to a grown-up who will act as referee, memorises it and then puts it back in the bag. This person is the splasher. The splasher fills up the container with water and the other players form a circle around him or her, though not too close.

Each of the surrounding players takes it in turn to choose a number and say it out loud to everyone. Once that number has been chosen, it is removed from the bag so it cannot be repeated – the next player must say a different number.

As soon as a player shouts out the number which was memorised by the splasher, the splasher throws the water at him or her, hopefully soaking the correct player but quite likely splashing a few others in the process.

If, however, none of the players in the circle shout out the number picked by the splasher, then the splasher must pour the water over his or her head, which is even funnier!

The Human Sink

This is a great energetic game for a scorching day on the beach for adults and children alike. And a fun way to cool down too. You'll just need two buckets, two large plastic bottles and two small plastic cups.

Nominate two players to be the human 'sinks'. Divide the remaining players into two teams and get them to line up one behind the other about five to ten metres from the sink – depending on how energetic everyone is feeling. Place a bucket full of water and a plastic cup in front of the first player in each line.

The human sinks then sit down in line with their team, each holding the plastic bottle upright on their head. On the word 'go', the first player from each team dunks the plastic cup in the water, runs to the sink and tries to pour the water into the bottle – kids like to miss quite a lot so that they can soak the human sink. When they have emptied the cup they race back to their line and hand the cup to the next player who repeats the action. The teams carry on until the bucket is empty or the bottle is full – you can decide which wins.

Beachcombing

Beachcombing arrived in Britain in the eighteenth century with the seaside holiday – the preserve of wealthy families who began to visit coastal spas because of their rejuvenating qualities. Only the upper classes could afford the time and the money for such trips – getting to the seaside might take days by horse-drawn carriage.

The resorts flourished over the next century, and the arrival of train travel in the 1850s, and bank holidays twenty years later, put seaside expeditions within the reach of many more people.

'Beachcombing' is perhaps the wrong word to describe what it represents: it suggests concentrated activity whereas it usually involves a meandering walk along the shoreline, picking up and putting back detritus washed up from the sea. Occasionally a memento is taken home – some driftwood or seaglass (bottle glass worn smooth by the ocean) – but usually beachcombing is an idle diversion.

Sophisticated recreational beachcombers might study storm patterns and ocean currents, and some use more tangible instruments to assist the discovery of rarer, exotic treasures. After the Second World War, a surplus of mine detectors was snapped up by relic hunters and soon the beachcombing metal detector became an eccentric figure on our coastal plains and in classified newspaper ads, hoovering the shifting surface for buried treasure hauls of lost coins, jewellery and assorted valuables not corroded beyond value by the saltwater.

Beachcombing is as much fun now as it ever was, and can easily be turned into a simple but delightful game, a Beach Scavenger Hunt, for children on holiday – perhaps for one of those days when the summer weather isn't all that you hope for and you want to keep warm while staying on the beach.

Beach Scavenger Hunt

Players are given a list of items to search for and collect on the beach. Obviously the list should be tailored for the surroundings – there's no point asking children to collect seashells if none are being washed up!

Things to find might include some of the following: a piece of driftwood, some seaweed, a white stone, a black stone, a speckled stone, a flower, a feather, a piece of string, a pearly shell, a white shell, a smooth piece of coloured glass, a red stone – and so on.

The game can be made into a competition by making the player who collects all of the items, or the most, in a set time, the winner. Or players could be divided into teams to hunt for the beach treasure together.

Whichever method is decided upon, remember to dress in suitable clothing and especially consider what you're going to wear on your feet – if you are going to be negotiating slippery rocks, it goes without saying that footwear with a good grip is essential. Don't wear clothes which are going to restrict your movement. Remember to think about how the tides and temperature may change during your Scavenger Hunt – particularly if you get distracted by something worth examining for a while. Bring a backpack for provisions, and for additional clothing or a swimsuit.

Beach Hopscotch

The origins of this classic children's game are lost in the mists of time, though some theories suggest that it was brought over to Britain by the Romans who taught British children how to play.

Whatever the truth of its origins, it is clear that it has been played
for many hundreds of years. Most often you see the hopscotch
grid marked out on the playground or on the pavement but we
used to play for hours on Kenneggy Beach in Cornwall. And it is
ideally suited to playing on a good sandy beach because when you
throw the stone or shell it doesn't roll on frustratingly out of the
box you've aimed for! So this version of the game is
for beaches.

Mark out the grid in the sand – it's good to use sand
down by the water as it will still be quite wet and will
not scuff up so much as dry sand once you start
jumping and hopping through the boxes. Finish it off
by drawing a picture of an ice cream or something
treat-like in the final box. The grid shown here is a
twelve-box one but if you want a shorter grid you can
make it eight. The only requirement is that there is a
pattern of one square and two squares that requires you
to alternately hop and jump with one and two feet.

Find a nice shell, flat pebble or stone (one that won't
roll or bounce when you throw it) and decide who is
going to go first – you could just get everyone to try
to get the closest throw to the final square.

The first player then starts his or her 'inning'. She
throws her stone into square number 1 and jumps over
this square so that no part of her foot touches it, and
carries on to the end of the 'grid', hopping on one foot
into the single squares and jumping with two feet (one
in either square) for the double squares side by side.
When she reaches the last square, the player turns
around and repeats the actions until she gets to square
number 2 when she bends down, picks up the stone in
square number 1 and jumps out of the grid without
touching square number 1. If she is successful with that she
continues, throwing her stone into square 2 and repeats the game,
this time not stepping in this square as she jumps. If she misses the
square with her throw or, when hopping, over- or under-steps and
lands in the forbidden square, then she is 'out'. Her stone remains in
the square she missed, until it is her turn again. Play passes to the
next player. The winner is the person who manages to complete all
twelve stages first.

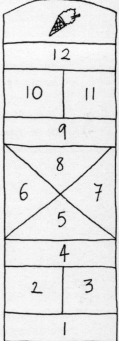

The game of course gets trickier as the higher squares are reached and it becomes harder to get the stone to land in the correct square.

As in tennis, if a player's stone lands on a line of the square they are aiming for, it is considered 'in'. But if a player lands on any of the lines when she is jumping, then she is out and the next player can start her innings.

Kites

The word 'kite' comes from an old English word 'cyta' which was used to mean 'bird', and kites have been instrumental in the development of man's attempts to fly. George Cayley (sometimes called the Father of Aeronautics) used kites to design what has been described as the first flying machine – a glider built in 1804 which was basically a kite mounted on a pole – and later in the same century, one of the pioneers of manmade flight, Lawrence Hargrave, used four box kites to lift himself sixteen feet off the ground.

There is something elemental about watching and controlling a kite flying high in the sky on a blustery spring day – and there's the excitement of discovering whether your own design can withstand the forces of nature high above you. Kites are fairly straightforward to construct and, of course, great fun to decorate as well. The simple instructions below are tried and trusted.

Make a Diamond Kite

You'll need

Two 6mm dowel or bamboo rods – one 90cm long and the
    other 60cm
String or garden twine
Glue – both strong wood glue and a paper glue
Material for the sail: brown paper, crêpe paper or a light muslin cloth
Ruler, pencil, scissors and sharp utility knife
Needle and thread
Elastic – about 50cm
Some fishing line or lightweight strong cord – 50m (or less)
    for the kite line
Ribbons, or long strips of plastic cut from bags, to decorate – each
    one up to 1m

The two wooden dowels form a cross – these are the 'spars' that are the backbone of your kite. Arrange these so that the shorter spar crosses the longer exactly a third of the way from the top. Mark each stick at this point with the pencil.

To have a successful kite, balance is key: make sure that your measurements are accurate and that the rods are precisely positioned – if they are not, your kite will pull to the side.

Now use the knife to make a small hollow from each spar at the cross point, so that they will fit tightly together.

Put a blob of wood glue in each hollow, fit the spars together and leave to dry. Then lash them together tightly using a length of twine

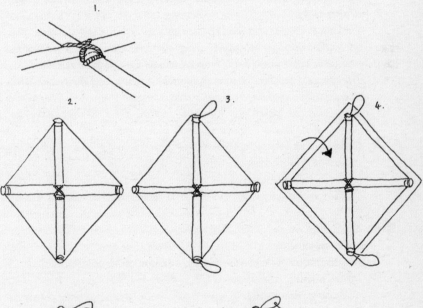

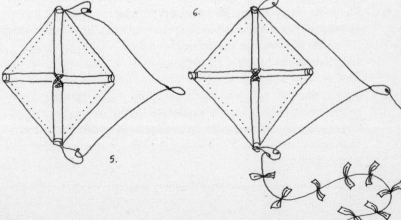

– lash them diagonally as shown in fig 2 on the previous page and cover the 'knot' with another small blob of glue to hold the frame secure.

Cut a narrow notch at the ends of each of the rods. This is to thread twine around the frame so that you can stick the 'sail' material to it. Take about 150cm of twine and secure it tautly around the frame (preferably with just one knot) – but take care not to pull it so tightly that it bends the frame. Make two loops from 15cm of the nylon cord and attach these to the top and bottom of the longest spar.

You can use any number of materials for the sail. Tissue paper is sometimes advised, but it's a bit too delicate. For a sturdier kite, use a good crêpe or brown paper, or a piece of light cotton muslin or similar fabric.

Lay your paper or material out on a flat surface and press or smooth it so it has no creases. Place the kite frame on the material, and use a ruler and pencil to draw round the outer edge of the frame, allowing a 3cm margin to act as a hem. Cut out the fabric or paper.

If you are using paper, simply fold the hem round the edges of the frame and use paper glue to secure, leaving the loops at the top and bottom free. Make sure the paper is pulled nicely taut across the kite frame as you stick. If you are using material it is better to sew it quite tightly around the twine using a needle and thread.

Next you need to create a 'bridle', which is a means of securing the kite to the kite line (the string by which you fly the kite). The bridle is adjustable so that the kite can be flown more efficiently depending on the wind speed. Make a hole halfway between the cross-spar and the top of the kite in both the spar and the sail. Then make another hole about 38–40cm below the cross-spar. Take a piece of elastic and thread it through both holes, tying a knot about 30cm away from the kite itself. Make sure that you create a loop at the point where you tie the knot so that there is something for the kite line to attach to.

Another essential component is the tail. The length of the tail helps you control the kite's performance. At its longest it needs to be about five times the height of the kite but should be constructed in sections so that you can adjust the length. If, for example, the kite is not holding steady once it's in the air, the tail is too short. If the kite won't get off the ground, then it is too long. A basic tail can be made using about a metre of string, to which you can add sections as appropriate.

Decorate the tail by tying on small lengths of ribbon, spaced roughly 10cm apart.

Next you need to attach the kite line to the loop you've made in the bridle. The line itself is best wound around a solid chunk of wood or plastic – something that is comfortable to grip when you are flying the kite high up in the air. Make sure, as you wind the line around the piece of wood, that there are no hitches in the string and that it can therefore be let out smoothly once the kite is airborne.

Finally, decorate the kite using paints or crayons, both front and back, according to whatever design you fancy. Go wild and enjoy it!

Two Kite-Flying Records

On 4th October 2003, the wonderfully named Mix McGraw set a new Guinness World Record by flying 230 stunt kites at one time. The record took place at the Air Force Museum at Wright-Patterson Air Force Base in Dayton, Ohio, and the train of kites measured 192 feet.

In July 2009, 3,710 children from Gaza set a new record of the most kites flown simultaneously.

Games to Play When Out on a Walk

Human Showjumping

A game for the grown-ups, or older children with longer legs.

When you're out on a long country walk, you can add a little competitive edge to your ramble by challenging your fellow walkers to a game of Human Showjumping. It's a simple notion but a distracting one: the aim of the game is to perform the most elaborate and intricate jumps over gates, puddles, ditches, creeks, cow pats, rocks and so on. You won't need anything for this except a vaulting imagination.

Points are awarded for creativity, style and execution and it'll have you thinking between gates and other obstacles about how you are going to tackle the next one.

For smaller children – if vaulting isn't an option – then suggest a race to see who can get to the other side the quickest and, again, award points for unusual moves. For really small children, a dog lead can make a useful rein to control the parent 'horse'.

One small piece of advice – if you are planning to do this, remember to wear trainers rather than wellies. Gate jumping in wellies is pretty difficult, though they offer better protection against bruises.

Disc Golf (or Frolf)

This is golf without exorbitant membership fees, stuffy dress codes or, indeed, clubs. A great game for when you're out and about on a walk, especially on the beach.

You'll need a Frisbee – either one for each player or just a single one to share. Bear in mind that Frisbees may go astray in the course of the walk.

As you walk along, each player takes it in turn to pick an object (or hole) to throw the frisbee to. You agree the number of throws you all think it should take and then each player throws the Frisbee, trying to reach the object in the agreed number of throws or fewer.

Unbelievably, some people take this happy diversion seriously, and there are even three different types of disc equating to putters, irons and drivers! You can get serious if you want to but if you just want a fun diversion on a walk, an ordinary Frisbee should do just fine.

Bark Rubbing

Bark or tree rubbing is a great way to get children to look at and try to distinguish different types of trees while out on a walk.

Sometimes the bark patterns are wonderfully ornate and with the application of an artistic eye can lend themselves to lovely wall art or unusual wrapping paper. Or, for the budding naturalists amongst you, why not keep an album of the rubbings you have made so that you can compare the different textures of the same trees during the seasons.

Making a bark rubbing couldn't be simpler. All you need to do is fix a piece of plain paper – nothing as thin as newsprint and nothing as thick as card but anything in between will do – to the trunk of the tree at a position where the bark makes a lovely pattern. You can fix the paper with masking tape and if you have young children you might want to hold the piece of paper in place for them.

You can either then use the full length of a wax crayon (take the paper wrap off the middle of the crayon so you can rub lengthways) or a stick of charcoal or, for finer drawings, a pencil to make the rubbing – simply apply an even pressure across the drawing instrument you are using. Don't rub too hard or you'll tear the paper. If you want you can of course also use different colours.

Leaf Rubbing

It's also a nice idea to make rubbings of the leaves to accompany your impression of the bark. With these it is best to collect the leaves and take them home; place your leaves on a piece of newspaper and lay the bark rubbing over the top. You create the leaf rubbing in exactly the same way as the bark rubbing – just be careful where you position the leaves relative to the bark so they don't overlap.

Blackberry Picking

So up we'd go to the wilder end of the valley, to the bramble-entangled Scrubs, bearing baskets and buckets and flasks of cold tea, like a file of foraging Indians. Blackberries clustered against the sky, heavy and dark as thunder, which we plucked and gobbled, hour after hour, lips purple, hands stained to the wrist.

Laurie Lee, *Cider With Rosie*

There really is little more satisfying than spending a golden autumn day in the brambles grabbing handfuls of blackberries. Generally they start to get ready for picking in late August or early September depending on how hot the summer has been and by early October, as a rule of thumb, they are past it. Traditionally 29th September is the day the Devil spits on blackberries, making them inedible.

If you're intending to eat as you go, wait for a good dry spell – rainwater on the berries tends to diminish their flavour a little. You'll need to take some plastic containers (or the more traditional punnets if you have any – on the whole they are easier to carry) and perhaps some thin gardening gloves for the more aggressive brambles. Pick your spot and harvest! Make sure that you (and others blackberrying with you) are careful about which berries you pick: if the berries aren't ripe, then leave them for someone else to pick later in the month. Blackberries grow so abundantly there's no need to worry about not getting enough.

If you're planning to eat them as soon as you get back, you'll find that they last a day or two but otherwise, blackberries freeze exceedingly well – just give them a good wash when you get home and divide them into bags according to how much you'll need for whichever recipe you intend to make. The prospect of digging out some blackberries on a gloomy Sunday in the depths of February provides at least one thing to look forward to in that grimmest of months.

Summer Flowers

NOSEGAYS, OR 'TUSSIE-MUSSIES'

OPHELIA: *There's rosemary, that's for remembrance; pray you, love, remember. And there is pansies, that's for thoughts.*

Hamlet, Act 4, Scene 5

Because of their immediate impact on the senses of sight, smell and touch, flowers have been used symbolically since ancient times. Dating back to the Middle Ages, 'tussie-mussies', also known as 'nosegays', were small, aromatic bouquets of flowers and herbs, which were carried to keep at bay the unpleasant odours of everyday life, and were even thought to prevent infections. Even today, judges at the Old Bailey carry a 'tussie-mussie' into the court several times each year – a tradition from Elizabethan times which was meant to guard against the spread of typhus, or 'gaol fever', from infected prisoners.

The Victorians, perhaps because of the strict conventions of the time, used tussie-mussies to convey sentiments they dared not utter in public. In the nineteenth century, dozens of dictionaries of floriography were compiled – the language or symbolism of flowers. It was quite important that the sender and receiver of flower 'messages' used the same dictionary, or else meanings might easily get confused with disastrous consequences.

These meanings could be very subtle and were by no means always positive, as they tend to be when we give flowers today, as you can see in the list which follows. For instance, you could signify hatred of someone by sending him or her an orange lily. A stinging nettle might imply that they were merely spiteful – saying it with flowers, indeed.

In those days, a great variety of wild flowers and plants grew in the countryside as well as being cultivated in gardens and parks. Many species have disappeared since then and we rely more on imported cut flowers for our gifts and displays, but it is still possible to find enough common plants to make one of the simple nosegays outlined below.

Making a Tussie-Mussie

If you're out on a walk in the country why not suggest to everyone (including younger children) that they collect some wild flowers to make a tussie-mussie with when you get back. You could 'interpret' what the meaning of the flowers people have collected using the language of flowers glossary overleaf.

You'll need some string or a ribbon, a sheet of kitchen roll or other absorbent paper and some tin foil.

Your aim is to arrange the plants together to compose a message in the language of flowers. Alternatively, you could just make an attractive posy to give to a grandparent, a mother in need of cheering up, or a special loved one. In either case, there are a couple of simple rules for making a small tussie-mussie.

Firstly, use just one central flower. Surround this with smaller blooms, and then sprigs of herbs and larger plants to frame and display the central arrangement to its best. Secondly, don't overcrowd the posy – simple really is more beautiful and allows the flowers to show at their best, rather than getting lost in the crowd.

If you do want to convey a message, study the list following for the meanings of various flowers, according to the Victorians. Be sure to give a list of the meanings to the receiver, who may have no idea what the different plants signify! But you may just have to make do with what's in the garden or sitting in a vase in the living room.

Secure your posy with loosely tied string, and then wrap the base of the stems in some damp kitchen paper. Wrap the base in a small strip of foil, to keep the damp paper in place. Tie a ribbon or string round the foil to finish the posy.

Flower Meanings

(from *The Language of Flowers*, or *Flora Symbolica*, by John Ingram)

Azalea – Temperance
Basil – Hatred
Bay leaf – I change but in death
Bindweed, small – Humility
Bluebell – Constancy. Sorrowful regret
Borage – Bluntness
Bramble – Lowliness. Envy. Remorse
Broom – Humility. Neatness
Burdock – Importunity. Touch me not
Buttercup – Ingratitude. Childishness
Cabbage – Profit
Carnation – Alas! For my poor heart
Carnation, pink – Woman's love
Carnation, striped – Refusal
Carnation, yellow – Disdain
Cherry blossom – Insincerity
Clover, four-leafed – Be mine
Clover, red – Industry
Coriander – Hidden worth
Corn – Riches
Cornflower – Delicacy
Cowslip – Pensiveness. Winning grace. Youthful beauty
Cress – Stability. Power
Daffodil – Regard. Unrequited love
Daisy – Innocence
Dandelion – Rustic oracle
Fennel – Strength
Fern – Fascination. Magic. Sincerity
Furze, or gorse – Love for all seasons. Anger
Geranium – Deceit
Gladioli – Ready armed
Grass – Submission. Utility

Hawthorn – Hope
Holly – Foresight
Hyacinth – Sport. Game. Play
Hydrangea – A boaster
Iris – Message
Ivy – Friendship. Fidelity. Marriage
Jasmine – Amiability
Jasmine, yellow – Grace and elegance
Lady's slipper – Capricious beauty. Win me and wear me
Lavender – Distrust
Lettuce – Cold-heartedness
Lily, white – Purity. Sweetness
Lily of the valley – Return of happiness. Unconscious sweetness
London pride – Frivolity
Marigold – Grief
Mint – Virtue
Mistletoe – I surmount difficulties
Mock orange – Counterfeit
Morning glory – Affectation
Moss – Maternal love
Nettle, common stinging – You are spiteful
Oak leaves – Bravery
Pansy – Thoughts
Parsley – Festivity
Pea, sweet – Departure
Peony – Shame. Bashfulness
Peppermint – Warmth of feeling
Petunia – Your presence soothes me
Poppy, red – Consolation
Primrose – Early youth and sadness
Raspberry – Remorse
Rhubarb – Advice
Rocket – Rivalry
Rose – Love
Rose, yellow – Decrease of love. Jealousy
Rosemary – Remembrance
Rudbeckia – Justice
Rue – Disdain
Sage – Domestic virtue
Salvia, blue – Wisdom

Snapdragon – Presumption, also 'No'
Snowdrop – Hope
Sorrel – Affection
Spearmint – Warmth of sentiment
Speedwell – Female fidelity
St John's Wort – Animosity
Strawberry blossoms – Foresight
Sunflower, tall – Haughtiness. False riches
Thistle, common – Austerity. Independence
Thyme – Activity or courage
Tulip, red – Declaration of love
Tulip, variegated – Beautiful eyes
Tulip, yellow – Hopeless love
Verbena, scarlet – Unite against evil
Verbena, white – Pray for me
Violet, blue – Faithfulness
Violet, yellow – Rural happiness

DAISY CHAINS

That well by reason men it call may
The daisie, or els the eye of the day,
The emprise, and floure of floures all.

Chaucer, Prologue to *The Legend of Good Women*, line 183

The common daisy (*Bellis perennis*) is, in our humble opinion, one of
the prettiest and most undervalued of flowers, and not just because
our beloved grandmother shared the name.

From early spring to late summer, these elegant white and yellow
jewels perfectly complement the green lawn grass. The 'day's eye'
opens and closes with the rising and setting sun, bringing a simple,
sunny joy to the smallest garden or largest park.

Their profusion also means that picking them is not a garden
crime, which is great news for children of all ages who like to make
daisy chains.

How to make a Daisy Chain
Simply take a daisy and make a hole in the stem with a fingernail.
Children are very good at this – small fingernails! Push the next
daisy through the slit and repeat the process until you have a chain of

flowers which can be tied together. The chain can now be worn as a bracelet – for arm or leg – or even as a little crown.

Variation: If you are lucky enough to have buttercups growing in your lawn as well as daisies, then interweave the flowers together to make a beautiful garland.

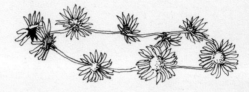

COLLECTING, PRESSING AND AIR DRYING FLOWERS

Pressing flowers was almost an art form in the Victorian era, and every expedition or picnic would have been an opportunity to capture flora at its best and keep it that way. Our mother was a fiend for pressing flowers, if that doesn't sound a bit strong, and we'd come across finely dried specimens in the pages of the most unlikely books.

We've included instructions below on how to build a simple flower press, though you can, of course, use the age-old 'press-in-a-book' method which works well if you follow these simple tips.

Flower Pressing Tips: Most flowers can be pressed – common sense will tell you what's likely to work well. Generally this means smaller blooms, or more delicate flower heads. For larger blooms, such as some roses, air drying may be a better option (see Air Drying on page 92). The best time to pick flowers for pressing is when it's dry and warm outside.

Place flowers or leaves of a similar size and thickness on a sheet of absorbent paper, like blotting paper, and make sure that no parts are overlapping. Place another sheet of the paper carefully on top of the flowers, and then place the two sheets in the middle of a heavy book, or some similar object, where they will be subjected to constant pressure.

If the flowers are more fleshy, you may have to change the blotting paper over the first few days – check to see how they are drying out.

Most plants will take between one and three weeks to dry out properly. Then you can use them for all sorts of decorative purposes.

Making a Flower Press

If you're feeling a little more adventurous, you can make your
own simple flower press.

You'll need

Two pieces of wood (plywood, or other), measuring about
    30cm by 30cm
Ten squares of thick cardboard, trimmed to the size of the
    wood press
Twenty sheets of blotting paper
Four 10cm screws, with wing nuts and washers
A drill

Firstly, drill a hole in the four corners of each plywood square – the
holes should be in the same place for each square, so that the screws
will go smoothly through each corner.

The cardboard sheets and blotting paper should be trimmed to fit
between the plywood squares. Cut a small triangle off the corners
of the cardboard and blotting paper, so the screws don't touch them
when they are inserted into the wood.

Now lay the cardboard sheets and blotting paper sheets between
the wooden squares – two pieces of blotting paper between each
piece of cardboard.

Finally, push the screws through the holes on the underside of the
press, and secure them with the washers and wing nuts on the top.
Your press is now ready for use.

To press flowers, undo the screws, remove the top wooden square
and all but the bottom cardboard sheet and bottom sheet of blotting
paper. Place your flowers carefully on the blotting paper, cover with
another sheet of blotting paper, and then a sheet of cardboard. Insert
your next piece of blotting paper and then your next specimen, and
repeat this process until you have finished. Then tighten the screws
to 'press' the flowers between the absorbent sheets.

The press can, of course, be made to a larger or smaller size,
depending on what plants you think you're likely to collect.
Similarly, more sheets can be inserted between the wooden squares.

To Air Dry Flowers

Air drying flowers works well for many larger specimens like
cornflowers, foxgloves, teasels, hydrangeas and roses. Pick the flowers
when they are fully grown and dry, as any dew or raindrops in the

petals or leaves may cause the plant to become mouldy before it is dried out properly.

To air dry them, hang the plants in small bunches and upside down in a warm, airy room, preferably without exposing them to strong light which may cause the colours to fade. It may take two or three weeks for the plants to dry out properly, at which point they should be quite brittle.

Marbles

On yon gray stone, that fronts the chancel door,
Worn smooth by busy feet now seen no more,
Each eve we shot the marble through the ring,
When the heart danced, and life was in its spring.

From *The Pleasures of Memory* by Samuel Rogers

Marbles have been played for centuries but are quite out of fashion now. A shame as it is a great game for developing hand–eye coordination and some of the old marbles themselves are quite beautiful.

Children would treasure their collection of marbles and keep them in a tin or bag, prizing some as their special marbles. Traditionally the marble games described below would be played for keeps; in other words, a player would keep an opponent's marbles if they had been fairly won in a game. This certainly adds a fiercely competitive edge to any game.

The terminology of marbles is quite charming. A 'taw' is the name given to the better-quality, stronger marbles while 'clays' are the cheap, penny variety. Players can shoot their marble by either 'trolling', 'hoisting', 'knuckling down' or 'fulking'. Every game begins with a competition to see who can get their marble closest to an agreed target – this is called 'lagging'.

There are many games that can be played – the most famous is Ringer which is described below.

There are several different techniques for aiming and shooting your marble, and in time you'll find your preferred method. Most common techniques are trolling, hoisting and knuckling down.

Trolling: Simply aim and throw your marble along the ground towards your target.

Hoisting: From a standing position, the marble is shot from knee level or higher at the target.

Knuckling down: Knuckling down is the most popular method and the most accurate, but the hardest to get the hang of.

Curl your fingers and cradle the marble in the crook of your curled index finger. Flex the index finger to hold the marble steady.

To 'knuckle down', place the knuckle and flat of your index finger on the ground and then use your thumb to flick the marble out of the crook.

With practice you will be able to increase the force and accuracy of your aim.

Ringer

This is the classic game of marbles. A circle of one metre in diameter is drawn on the ground with chalk, for example, and this is the playing area. A single marble is placed in the middle and from that four arms are marked out (in directions north, south, east and west) using two marbles on each arm placed at seven cm intervals. These marbles are called 'ducks'. So the final shape is of a cross made up of marbles with seven cm gaps between them.

Whoever wins the lag (the mini-game to decide who goes first) has first shot and must attempt to knock any of the ducks out of the ring. If he is successful (and his shooter remains in the ring) he gets another go from wherever the shooter came to rest.

Each duck knocked out of the ring counts as a point. If the shooter also rolls out of the ring that is the end of that player's turn. If that player fails to knock a duck out of the ring and his shooter remains in the

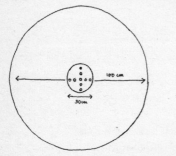

ring, it is the end of his turn and the next and subsequent players can attempt to knock his shooter out of the ring. If they succeed they get all the points and marbles that the previous shooter had accumulated to that point.

The aim of the game is to have the most points when the last marble is knocked out of the ring.

Tip: A marble 'pro' once told us that the thing to bear in mind is not just that you shoot other marbles but that you concentrate on the position of your marble so that you have a good next shot – just like in pool or snooker.

Picking the Plums

A line is drawn along the ground and each player places as many marbles as he wants along the line, spacing them about four inches apart. An offing line is agreed and each player takes it in turns to try to shoot marbles from the line.

If no marble is hit, the next player takes his turn. If a marble is hit out of the line, he collects that marble and takes another shot. The player continues to shoot and collect marbles as he dislodges them, until he misses. Play continues with players taking turns in order, until all the plums have been picked.

The player who gains the most marbles is the winner.

The Castle

Form a kind of pyramid, with three marbles set in a triangle, and a fourth balanced on top; or make a base of six, then balance four more on top and one last marble on the top.

Draw a circle round the pyramid of marbles. One player takes the post of keeper or guard – his job is to rebuild the castles as they fall. The other players take it in turns to shoot from an agreed distance (make an 'offing' line if that helps); if the shooter manages to drive out marbles from the ring he is entitled to as many marbles from the guard as he shot out. The guard rebuilds the castle for the next player until it is agreed to swap over.

Three Holes

Make three holes in the ground, about four feet apart, either in a line, or at each point of a triangle. Mark an offing roughly seven feet from the first hole.

The aim of the game is for each player to get his marbles into each hole sequentially and back to the beginning again. If one player shoots a marble into a hole, he can take another turn and try to get his next marble into the next hole – or try to knock his opponent away from a hole. If he succeeds in knocking an opponent's marble out of the way, he may still try to score in the next hole. After 'gaining' a hole, at his next turn he should shoot from about a hand's span away from that hole. If he misses, the second player tries his fortune, each shooting by turns, as his opponent fails.

The sequence is usually: first hole, second hole, third hole, second, first, second, third. In tougher times than these the winner used to be able to shoot marbles at his opponent's knuckles – a prize, apparently. It's more common now to play for a stake of marbles.

Knockout

This is a simple game that only requires a wall. Any number can play – in fact the more the better.

One player throws his marble against the wall, aiming for it to bounce not more than three feet back from it. The next player again bounces his marble against the wall and tries to hit the first player's marble or get within an agreed distance of it. If he succeeds then he wins the first player's marble; if not, play passes to the next player who tries to hit the second player's marble. If he succeeds then he wins all the marbles thrown so far. And so on.

If there are only two players it is often best to have two or three rounds so that the stakes are higher.

Conkers

Although conkers is a game for two players, it is also a spectator sport – one of the first occasions for children to learn the joys and perils of humiliation. The two players, each with a conker threaded onto a piece of string, take turns hitting each other's conker using their own until one breaks.

Conkers has been around a while, but maybe not as long as you'd think. The first recorded game using the nuts of the horse chestnut tree (which are the 'conkers') was on the Isle of Wight in 1848.

The name comes from the dialect word conker, meaning hard

(related to French *conque*, meaning a conch). The name may also
be influenced by the verb *conquer*, as the game was also called
conquerors. Conkers are also known regionally as obblyonkers,
cheggies or cheesers.

Roald Dahl said, 'A great conker is one that has been stored in a
dry place for at least a year. This matures it and makes it rock hard
and therefore formidable.' However, the Campaign for Real Conkers
claimed that hardening conkers should be regarded as cheating, and
cheating, they said, was causing a drop in interest in the game. How
Very British.

Whatever your opinion, there are few more traditional British
pastimes than a good game of conkers.

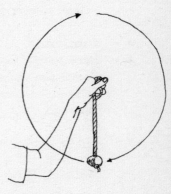

How to Play Conkers

The aim of the game is, simply, to destroy rather than be destroyed. In
other words, to smash your opponents' conkers to smithereens.
Select your conker – choose one which is solid, firm and undamaged.

Make a hole through the middle of the conker, using a skewer or
drill, and thread a long piece of string through it, tying a double or
triple knot at the bottom and above the conker to secure.

Now – do battle with your opponent.

Decide who gets first strike. If you are lucky enough to go first,
you get to choose the height at which your opponent must hold
their conker.

Draw back your conker, with the string wrapped round your hand
several times to shorten it, and holding it taut, take aim to strike.
Release and swing to strike your opponent's conker, as hard as you
possibly can.

Three strikes and you are out – in other words, you have three attempts to hit your target. If not, it is your opponent's turn to strike.

If you score a direct hit, then it is also your opponent's turn to strike your conker. (Unless, of course, you destroyed the opposition's conker first go, in which case, 'Well done!')

There are a couple of extra rules: If you hit your opponent's conker 'round the world' – causing it to do a full circle in the air – you get an extra go.

If the conker strings get intertwined, then the first player to shout out 'Strings!' gets an extra shot – no matter whose turn is next. The winner is the player who is 'conker intactica' when their opponent's conker has been smashed off the string.

You can then go on to face your next opponent. Traditionally, the winner in a contest adds the victories of their opponent's conker to their own tally. So, if your maiden conker smashes a conker which has beaten three foes, it has a total score of four – your victory plus your opponent's three victories – and is known as a 'fourer'. A certain amount of honesty is required because the temptation to intimidate with a 'fiftyer' may be hard to resist.

Whittling Sticks

Whittling can be immensely absorbing as a pastime and can produce very satisfying results. It's pretty simple to get started: you just need a sharp penknife and some wood. A lot of people start with twigs and small branches because they are easy to whittle and you can quickly achieve excellent results. Thereafter you can progress to more complex and complicated designs from blocks of wood.

There are a few basic tips that will help from the outset. As anyone who whittles or works with wood in any shape or form will tell you, you need to keep your knife sharp.

To start whittling you only need a few basics, namely a penknife (preferably with two blades – one maximum 3.5cm, the other 5–6cm; a sharpening stone or knife sharpener (there are many kinds to choose from); and some twigs or branches.

The comfort of the knife handle is important too: you'll be using it for long continuous periods so it has to feel right.

When selecting the wood it's best not to pick wood that is either too dry (i.e. it snaps if you try to bend it) or wood that is too green: you want it to have a little give in it but not too much. If you find a source of wood in the right condition, it can be kept in bags in the freezer to retain its moisture until you are ready to use it.

If possible the wood should also have the grain going in only one direction. If you are starting with blocks of wood rather than branches or twigs, choose balsa or other soft woods.

There are three basic strokes to master in whittling.

1. The first is used to take off larger chunks of wood. Holding the wood in your non-whittling hand, make long deep strokes away from your body with the knife. The wrist is usually firm to help make the cuts as effective as possible.

2. The second (the draw cut) is for finer work. The action is more like the one you use for peeling an apple – the movement is around the branch towards you. Brace the wood with the thumb from your cutting hand (while holding the wood with your non-cutting hand) and make sure that there is always some wood between the blade and your cutting-hand thumb! (See illustration.)

3. Thumb pushing is for precise, accurate work. You grip the knife with the fingers of your right hand (as if putting it inside a fist) and push down the blade with the thumb. The wood is held with the four fingers of the left hand while the left thumb pushes either the back of the blade or your right thumb (vice versa if you are left-handed).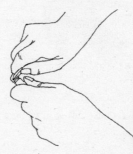

You are now ready to whittle!

GAMES ON THE GO

Long journeys by car, train or bus can either be a living nightmare or can pass relatively quickly with some laughter and good humour. We prefer the latter approach. These games are also great if one of the passengers suffers from travel sickness because looking out of the window – or at least not down at a book or DVD player screen – is the best way to avoid it.

Games for Journeys

I Spy

The simplest and most famous of all journey games is undoubtedly I Spy.
It's a very simple game which is great for familiarising young children with
the alphabet but can be enjoyed by passengers of any age. Even the driver
can join in.

The person to go first selects an object that they can see – either
in or out of the car – and then tells the other players the initial letter,
or letters, of the object in the following manner:

'I spy, with my little eye, something beginning with D.' (In this
case, a dog in the back window of a car.) The players then try to
guess what it is, and the first person to do so wins that round and
goes next. If the object disappears from view, because a car in front
speeds off or there are no cows in fields for a few minutes, then the
player must tell the guessers, 'I can't see it at the moment'. It's
therefore wise to pick something which is likely to reappear at some
stage! One other point to note: you should decide whether you are
going to allow objects with multiple initials, PS for petrol station, for
example. These are more fun and you can think up some really quite
ridiculous things to guess – GTOHM, or Girl Talking On Her
Mobile!

Pub Cricket

One person is put in to bat. Every time you travel past a pub, look at
the sign, or name of the pub, and see what kind of living creature is
on it. Then count the number of legs that animal has. So The
Cheshire Cat has four and the batsman scores four runs. If the sign
has no creature on it – say The Four Feathers, The Three Tuns or,
controversially, The King's Head – then the batsman scores no runs
and is out. The next player comes in to bat.

This game has the leisurely feel of a typical drawn-out local
cricket match and passes the time on a long journey through the
countryside perfectly.

If you're on the motorway you could change the run-scoring
method to wheels on different kinds of vehicles – it would be
impossible to count all of the cars (unless you're travelling late at
night) so restrict it to certain makes of car or types of vehicle. If you
pass a lorry with more than six wheels, your innings is over and
batting passes to the next player.

Number Plate LOL

An excellent game for the expert texters in the car. Simply take it in
turns to pick a car either ahead or behind or flashing past your car
on the other side of the road or motorway. Look at the three-letter
sequence on the number plate and call it out for your fellow passengers (the driver can join in now). Everyone then tries to come up
with the best three-word phrase using the letters as the initial letters
of the words in the style of abbreviated text speak. So VCL might be
Very Clever Loony or MLB My Little Brontosaurus. LOL indeed.

Train Journey Bingo

This game is a great one for train journeys. It can also be played in
the car but, as it involves reading a bingo card, be aware of the
potential for travel sickness. It needs a little advance preparation but
will keep passengers engaged on the longest journey – you can adapt
it for different age groups and different environments too, so it is
nice and flexible. Depending on your route, draw up a list of likely
objects or events you might see and give cards with identical lists of
those things, each with a tick box beside it, to all those playing. So,
for example, a journey through the countryside might generate the
following card:

Countryside Bingo:

☐ Grain silo
☐ Cows
☐ Railway tracks
☐ Pond or lake
☐ Bridge
☐ Tractor
☐ Wind turbine
☐ Horses
☐ Deer
☐ Barn
☐ Oak tree
☐ River

And so on. First person to tick all the boxes gets a treat of some sort.
Here are some ideas for city and suburban bingo:

City Bingo:

- ☐ Bus
- ☐ Ambulance with flashing light
- ☐ Advertising hoarding with a cat on it
- ☐ Dog
- ☐ Statue
- ☐ Railway tracks
- ☐ Person with pram
- ☐ Caravan
- ☐ Ice cream van
- ☐ Church
- ☐ Person talking on a mobile phone while driving

Suburbs Bingo:

- ☐ Church
- ☐ Flashing traffic light
- ☐ Food shop
- ☐ Cyclist
- ☐ School
- ☐ Church
- ☐ Park playground
- ☐ Bridge
- ☐ Dustbin lorry
- ☐ Post office
- ☐ Person walking a dog

Cow Counting

In fact, you can decide to count anything you like – we used to pick a type of car and count those as they sped past us on the other side of the motorway. The principle remains the same – pick a common sight (and adapt the object depending on where you're travelling) and start to keep a tally of how many you spot. To introduce an extra competitive element, you can add other things on to the spotting list and give them different point values. So, if you decide on cows as the object of the count, make them one point each; add in, say, a white horse at ten points, a windmill at twenty points and so on. If you divide the car into two teams (left and right side) that makes for a good rivalry. Finally, if you want to introduce a real edge, employ the 'Cemetery Wipeout' rule: if a cemetery appears on your side of the car then you lose all of your points BUT only if the opposing team shouts 'Cemetery Wipeout' when they spot it. Do agree before you start playing when you're going to stop (perhaps when one team reaches an agreed number of points or you play for a certain amount of time).

Christmas Trees

A seasonal variation of Cow Counting is for players to count lit Christmas trees on their side of the road. Extra points for any trees outside in a garden or in a town square. For purists (!), deduct points for trees with blinking fairy lights.

Yellow Car/Mini Car

A good game for long car or bus journeys, especially on motorways. Players must try to be first to spot a yellow car, or a Mini. Yellow vans don't count.

Yellow cars and Minis score five points.

Footballers' Initials

We used to play this endlessly – either in the car, on a walk or round the dinner table. It was one of those games that we just resorted to whenever we were bored. The idea couldn't be simpler. You pick a footballer, say his initials and the other players have to guess who you're thinking of. If the other players are finding it difficult, you can give clues, like the division he plays in, the colour of his team's strip and so on. First one to guess correctly is the winner and sets the next initials.

Capitals

Another stalwart of the dinner table and long journeys, capitals is great for helping children find out a little bit more about the world. You name a country and the other players have to name the capital city. You can give charade-type clues – 'Sounds like …'The first one to shout the right answer picks the next capital for the group to guess.

What Kind of Chocolate Bar am I?

A bit like 20 Questions but with a confectionery twist, this game is excellent for car journeys. One player thinks up the name of his or her favourite chocolate bar and announces, 'I am a chocolate bar.'

What kind of chocolate bar am I?' The other passengers must now
ask a series of questions to try to be the first to guess the name of
the chocolate bar in question. Answers can only be 'yes' or 'no'.
The kinds of questions asked are:

'Do you have nuts in?'
'Are you a wafer bar?'
'Are you solid chocolate all the way through?'
'Are you still being sold?' (If the players are of the same generation,
some nostalgic references to chocolate past is fun.)
'Can you be broken into squares?'
'Do you have a red wrapper?'

And so on. The person to guess correctly gets to think up the next
chocolate bar.

RAINY DAY GAMES

We all know the feeling. It's a wet weekend – spring, summer, autumn or winter. Outside the rain pours down, splattering the windows and rattling on the roof; you're going nowhere, but you still want to enjoy this precious time with your family, your friends.

Well, here's a fabulous selection of activities to make you forget about the drizzle including some real classics like Battleships, memory games and Bingo. There are also some great skills to learn – making paper aeroplanes, juggling, constructing a Victorian wonder-turner … enough excitement here to brighten up the dankest, dullest of days at any time of year.

Hand Games

Paper Rock Scissors

This very simple age-old favourite game for two or more players is often used as a way of determining who is It. The world over there are umpteen versions including *Cachipun, Jan-ken-pon, Kauwi-bauwi-bo,* and *Rochambeau.*

The players each decide secretly on one of three weapons:

★ Paper – indicated by holding your hand out flat with palm down.
★ Rock – hand made into a fist and held flat.
★ Scissors – index and middle finger splayed to indicate an open pair of scissors.

On the count of three, or after chanting, 'Paper-rock-scissors,' both players simultaneously display one hand in the form of the chosen weapon – paper, rock or scissors.

The winner is decided according to the following rules:

★ Paper wraps rock: paper wins.
★ Scissors cut paper: scissors wins.
   ★   Rock blunts scissors: rock wins.

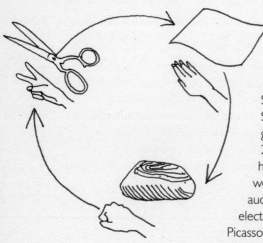

If the two same weapons are selected – rock meets rock, paper meets paper – the game is replayed until a winner is found.

Some consider Paper Rock Scissors to be more than just a game of chance. According to a 2005 BBC report, the auction houses Sotheby's and Christie's were both in the running for the auction of the Maspro Denkoh electronics corporation's $20 million Picasso and Van Gogh collection, but the firm's director could not decide which auction house to choose.

He settled on the idea that the paintings would be auctioned by whichever house won a single round of Paper Rock Scissors.

Sotheby's apparently trusted to luck but Christie's sought help from
two experts of the game – the eleven-year-old twin daughters of
one of its directors – who advised that most beginners decide that
rock 'feels' the strongest and therefore choose the weapon that
defeats rock – paper. They advised Christie's therefore to select
scissors. They did. Sotheby's chose paper and so lost the contract
to sell the paintings.

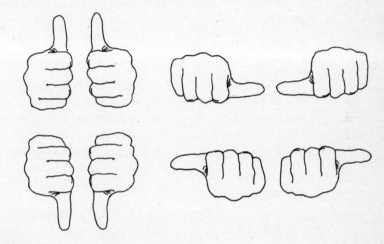

Thumbs Up

This is a variation of Simon Says, but with a twist – in fact, it's also
known as Sneaky Simon. It's played with thumbs performing the
opposite of whatever is instructed.

All players sit around a table with both hands on the table in front
of them.

Another, not playing, is Sneaky Simon and shouts out one of four
instructions:

Thumbs Up!
Thumbs Down!
Thumbs In!
Thumbs Out!

The players must immediately do the opposite of what they are told
with their thumbs – down instead of up, in instead of out, and so on.
Any hesitation or getting it wrong and the player is out.

The last player in is the winner and becomes Sneaky Simon.

Pen and Paper Games

Tapatan

Tapatan is a game of strategy for two players. It originated in the Philippines but versions of it are played all over the world. It's very similar to Noughts and Crosses in that the aim of the game is to get

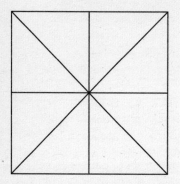

a row of three connected counters either horizontally, vertically or diagonally, on the points of the board.

Mark a simple board as shown in the illustration on a square of thick paper or card.

You need six counters: three counters of the same colour for each player, green for one player, yellow for the other. (You can make your own counters by cutting discs from coloured paper or card.)

To start the game, each player takes it in turn to place a single counter on one of the vacant points of the board.

Pieces may not be moved from these starting points until all six of the players' pieces have been placed.

On the next turn, the first player moves one of his counters, one space at a time, following the line of the board from one point to the next. Moves can be made horizontally, vertically and diagonally on the board until a row of three counters is formed.

Only one piece can be moved per turn, and counters cannot be jumped, i.e. moved, over another counter on the board.

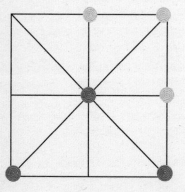

If a player is unable to make a move the game is a stalemate; and stalemate can also be declared if a counter is moved to the same position three times in succession.

The game is won when one player manages to connect three of his or her counters in a straight line on the board – sounds simple but it requires a lot of strategic thinking.

Nine Men's Morris (also called Mills or Merels)

This game for two players, thought to be a precursor to Noughts and Crosses, is one of the oldest games recorded in Britain. The 'boards' have been found scratched into the cloisters at Canterbury Cathedral and Westminster Abbey – some less than devout monks were clearly more interested in games of strategy than their prayers.

As in Tapatan, the aim is to create chains of three counters in a row – this is called 'a mill'. Each time a player creates a mill, he or she is entitled to take one of his opponent's pieces.

You'll need a board marked out as shown in the illustration below on a piece of card or paper and eighteen 'pieces' or coloured counters – nine of each colour.

The board has twenty-four points along which the players move their counters. To start the game, players take turns to place one counter on an intersection of the board – mills can be formed also at this stage.

Once all eighteen pieces are placed, players take turns to move one counter at a time in order to create a mill. When a player forms a mill, he or she can take one of their opponent's pieces from any part of the board. A player can only remove a piece from a formed mill when there are no other available pieces on the board.

Counters may only be moved along the horizontal and vertical lines (they cannot be moved diagonally) to an empty point on the board and a mill can only be formed on either the vertical or horizontal lines of the board.

The game continues with each player moving one piece at a time until no more moves are possible, or a player has only two pieces left.

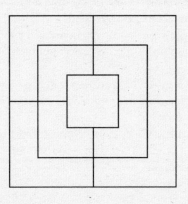
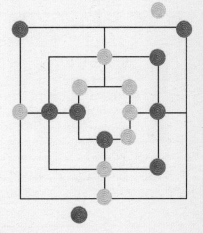

Battleships

Another classic game of strategy and guesswork, this one invented in the early part of the twentieth century. Apparently the inventor didn't patent the game – an oversight his relatives must be more than a little peeved about.

It's a game for two players of any age – each of whom has two identical grids. Normally this is ten by ten squares but it is very easy to play with other sized grids – just bear in mind that the bigger the grid, the longer the game will take to play. These days it is very simple to create grids using a spreadsheet program but it is more fun and (if you're playing with younger children) better for the players to mark out the grid and coordinates on a piece of paper themselves, marking letters A to J along the side axis and numbers 1 to 10 across the top.

On one of their grids, each player marks the positions of their battleships by blocking out the correct number of squares for each ship type as shown below. Usually there are five kinds of ship and they each take up a certain number of squares – placed either vertically or horizontally. These positions are the closely guarded secret of the game – you might want to stand a book between you and your opponent to prevent peeking. The ships cannot overlap, even at a corner, and the squares they occupy must be consecutive. Once marked it is as well for the player to write which kind of ship they are.

The other grid is for the player to record his or her shots at the enemy's fleet and is blank at the start of the game. Or you can decide together on your own variations of these formations and agree them in advance.

Ship Type	Number of Squares
aircraft carrier	5
battleship	4
destroyer	3
submarine	3
patrol boat	2

One player starts by calling out a coordinate (D7, for example). If that 'shot' has hit an opponent's ship, then the opponent must say so and should name the type of vessel. That square is then marked as being a hit by the caller. If the shot is a miss, that square is marked with an X. The turn passes to the other player who proceeds in the same way.

The game carries on until one player has destroyed the opposing fleet.

	1	2	3	4	5	6	7	8	9	10
A					X					
B						X				
C	O	X								
D	O							X		
E										
F								X	O	O
G				X						
H			X							
I						X				
J				X						

Variation: In the Salvo version of Battleships, each player may call as many shots as he or she has ships left. So the first player calls out five shots and is told how many hits he has made before the turn passes to his or her opponent. Once a player's ship has been sunk he or she gets one less shot.

Dots and Boxes

This very old, and deceptively simple, game of strategy is a bit like a cross between Connect 4 and Noughts and Crosses.

The aim is to complete full boxes within the grid, and at the same time to prevent your opponent from doing so.

On a piece of paper, draw a grid of dots – six by six, ten by ten or twenty by twenty, depending on the number of players and how long you want the game to last.

Each player takes it in turn to draw a line (either horizontal or vertical, but NOT diagonal) to join two neighbouring dots on the grid.

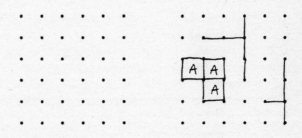

When a player successfully joins four dots to form a box, it is marked with their initials, and they can either draw a new line, or choose to let their opponent make the next move. If a player cannot form any more boxes, then play goes to the next player.

Players must think defensively in order to prevent an opponent forming a chain of boxes and running away with the game.

The player with the most complete boxes is the winner.

Sprouts

A player draws a small number of dots on a piece of paper – to begin with, start with two dots.

The first player then joins two dots, or one dot to itself, with a curve which cannot touch or cross any other curve or dot.

A new dot is then drawn on this new curve.

No dot can have more than three curves attached to it.

The game ends when no player can make a move. The last player to have drawn a curve is the winner.

As you become more familiar with this fascinating game of mathematical strategy, start with more dots on the page to play longer, more complicated, games of Sprouts.

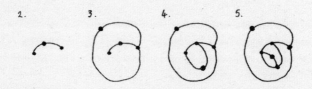

BINGO

Bingo, the classic game much loved by little old ladies all over our land, can in fact be a pretty ruthless game. It demands intense concentration and quick reactions.

Bingo is said to have originated in Italy in the sixteenth century before spreading to France and then finally to Britain. Part of the charm of the game is in the number-calling expressions which have developed over decades. Some are based on simple rhymes while others have some historical origin – for instance, 'Kelly's eye', meaning one, refers to one-eyed Australian bandit Ned Kelly. And some are distinctly bawdy.

Make your Own Bingo Game

The game is also fun for the kids to construct from card and other bits from the recycling bin.

You'll need a bingo card for each player – wide enough to hold nine columns and deep enough to hold three rows. (Cut-up old cereal boxes are perfect.)

You'll also need counters with the numbers 1 to 99 written on them – again you can make these using old bits of card or paper – a bag or hat from which to draw the numbers and fifteen blank counters per player to cover the numbers on the card that have been called. You can use chocolate buttons or other sweets instead of card for these.

You should agree before you start what the winning prize is – it's good to have something to aim for to increase the competitive tension in the room. Either everyone 'pays to play' in which case there is a pot to be collected at the end, or the hosts provide appropriate prizes.

First each player draws the grid on their card – the left-most column represents 1 to 10; the second 11 to 20, and so on.

The player then randomly chooses five numbers for each row (leaving four blank). See diagram below: this is a completed card ready to play.

A Completed Home-Made Bingo Card

1–10	11–20	21–30	31–40	41–50	51–60	61–70	71–80	81–90	91–100
3	14			43			73		92
		27	35		55	67		83	
	17		39	47		69			99

Once all the players have constructed their grids, the caller starts to call out the numbers picked at random from the bag. When a number is called that matches one of the random numbers a player has selected, he or she covers the number with one of the counters. The first player to cover all of his or her numbers shouts 'Bingo!' or 'Housie!' and takes the prize.

BINGO NUMBER NICKNAMES

Below is a list of just some of the Bingo caller's lingo.

1. Kelly's eye – Buttered scone – At the beginning – Little Jimmy – Nelson's column – B1 Baby of Bingo – First on the board – Number ace
2. One little duck – Baby's done it – Doctor Who – Me and you – Little boy blue – Home alone – Peek a boo
3. Dearie me – I'm free – Debbie McGee – You and me – Goodness me – One little flea – Cup of tea – Monkey on the tree
4. The one next door – On the floor – Knock at the door – Bobby Moore – Shut the door
5. Man alive – Jack's alive – One little snake
6. Tom mix – Tom's tricks – Chopsticks – In a fix
7. Lucky seven – God's in heaven – One little crutch – David Beckham – One hockey stick – A slice of heaven
8. Garden gate – Golden gate – At the gate – Harry Tate – One fat lady – She's always late – Sexy Kate – Is she in yet
9. Doctor's orders
10. Downing Street – Cock and hen – Uncle Ben – David's den (Number 10 has, over the years, used the names of various prime ministers) – A big fat hen
11. Legs eleven – Legs – They're lovely – Kelly's legs number eleven – Chicken legs – Skinny legs
12. One dozen – One and two – A dozen – Monkey's cousin (rhymes with 'a dozen') – One doz' if one can
13. Unlucky for some – Devil's number – Baker's dozen
14. Valentine's Day
15. Rugby team – Young and keen – Yet to be kissed
16. Sweet sixteen – She's lovely – Never been kissed
17. Often been kissed – Over-ripe – Old Ireland – Dancing queen – The age to catch 'em – Posh and Becks
18. Key of the door – Now you can vote – Coming of age
19. Goodbye teens
20. One score – Getting plenty – Blind twenty
21. Royal salute – Key of the door – If only I was – Just my age – At twenty-one watch your son
22. Quack quack – Two little ducks – Ducks on a pond – Dinky doo – All the twos – Bishop Desmond – Put your tutus on – Toot toot

23. A duck and a flea – Thee and me – The Lord's my shepherd (based on 23rd Psalm) – A duck on a tree
24. Two dozen – Did you score? – Do you want some more?
25. Duck and dive – At twenty-five, wish to have wife
26. Bed and breakfast (traditional price was two shillings and sixpence) – Half a crown (equivalent to two shillings and sixpence) – Pick and mix
27. Little duck with a crutch – Gateway to heaven
28. In a state – The old brags – Overweight – Duck and its mate
29. You're doing fine – In your prime – Rise and shine
30. Burlington Bertie – Dirty Gertie – Speed limit – Blind thirty – Flirty thirty – Your face is dirty
31. Get up and run
32. Buckle my shoe
33. Dirty knees – All the feathers – All the threes – Gertie Lee – Two little fleas – Sherwood Forest (all the trees)
34. Ask for more
35. Jump and jive – Flirty wives
36. Three dozen – Perfect (as in 36-24-36)
37. A flea in heaven – More than eleven
38. Christmas cake
39. Those famous steps – All the steps – Jack Benny
40. Two score – Life begins at – Blind forty – Naughty forty
41. Life's begun – Time for fun
42. That famous street in Manhattan – Winnie the Pooh
43. Down on your knees
44. Droopy drawers – All the fours – Open two doors
45. Halfway house – Halfway there
46. Up to tricks
47. Four and seven
48. Four dozen
49. PC (Police Constable – from *The Adventures of PC 49*) – Copper – Nick nick – Rise and shine
50. Bull's eye – Bung hole – Blind fifty – Half a century – Snow White's number (five-oh, five-oh …)
51. I love my mum – Tweak of the thumb – The Highland Div[ision]
52. Weeks in a year – The Lowland Div[ision] – Danny La Rue – Pack 'o cards
53. Stuck in the tree – The Welsh Div[ision] – The joker
54. Clean the floor – House of Bamboo (famous song)

55. Snakes alive – All the fives – Give us fives – Bunch of fives
56. Was she worth it?
57. Heinz varieties – All the beans (Heinz 57 varieties of canned beans)
58. Make them wait – Choo choo Thomas
59. Brighton line (engine 59 or it took 59 minutes to go from London to Brighton)
60. Three score – Blind sixty – Five dozen
61. Baker's bun
62. Tickety boo – Turn on the screw
63. Tickle me
64. The Beatles' number – Red raw
65. Old age pension – Stop work (retirement age)
66. Clickety click – All the sixes
67. Made in heaven – Argumentative number
68. Saving grace
69. The same both ways – Your place or mine? – Any way up – Either way up – Any way round
70. Three score and ten
71. Bang on the drum – Lucky one
72. A crutch and a duck – Six dozen – Par for the course (golf) – Lucky two
73. Crutch with a flea – Queen B – Under the tree – Lucky three
74. Candy store – Grandmamma of Bingo – Lucky four
75. Strive and strive – Big Daddy – Granddaddy of Bingo – Lucky five
76. Trombones – Seven 'n' six – Was she worth it? – Lucky six
77. Sunset strip – All the sevens – Two little crutches – The double hockey stick – Lucky seven
78. Heaven's gate – Lucky eight
79. One more time – Lucky nine
80. Gandhi's breakfast – Blind eighty – Eight and blank – There you go matey
81. Fat lady and a little wee – Stop and run – Corner shot
82. Fat lady with a duck – Straight on through
83. Fat lady with a flea – Time for tea – Ethel's ear
84. Seven dozen
85. Staying alive
86. Between the sticks
87. Fat lady with a crutch – Torquay in Devon
88. Two fat ladies – Wobbly wobbly – All the eights
89. Nearly there – All but one

90. Top of the shop – Top of the house – Blind ninety – As far as we go
    – End of the line

Paper Cricket

Paper Cricket is a simple paper version of the game we used to play
with special 'cricket' dice. There were two dice – the faces of one
showed ways of getting out and of the other runs scored.

   In this version, you make a paper 'wheel of fortune'. Cut a disc,
about 12cm in diameter, from a piece of thick paper or card, and
mark it in twelve sections (like pieces of a pie). Each of these wedges
represents the possible runs scored and means of getting out. So
write the following in one section each:

   '1', '2', '3', '4' '6' – possible number of runs scored

and:

   'LBW', 'Wicket', 'Stumped', 'Wide', 'No ball', 'Caught' – possible
   ways of getting out.

The pieces of pie don't have to be all the same size – their size could
reflect the frequency with which each 'event' happens (so '1' would
be bigger than 'stumped', for example).

   Push a pin or pencil through the centre of the disc so that it can
be spun.

   The players write out their teams on a piece of paper and agree
who is batting first.

   The player from the fielding side spins the disc (representing a ball
bowled) and the first batsman team player dabs down on the
spinning disc with his pencil.

   Wherever his pencil lands on the disc is the outcome of that ball
– 4 runs, or LBW, or Caught, for example – and is marked on his
score paper.

   Players can agree on a certain number of overs to be played before
the other side has its innings, or continue to play until the batting
team is all out before the other team bats.

   The team or player with the biggest total score takes the match.

Variation: The game can be as simple or as complicated as you
want to make it. Optional extras may be added to the disc, for
example, Wide, No Ball, or a Bye (one run for batting team and an
extra ball to bowled in the over).

Family Newspaper

This is a fantastic activity for holidays – particularly wet ones. A great way of filling up down time during the long summer months and a wonderful keepsake for years to come.

The idea is that the family or people holidaying together create a record of their time away (or indeed at home if you want to play this over the course of the school summer holidays) with every member contributing different aspects of what normally goes into a newspaper. Based on things that have happened and perhaps imagined consequences, a lot of stories, adverts, events, reminders etc. are entered into a book – either with photos or drawings or pictures cut out of magazines – which serves as the record of that holiday.

Drawing Games

Five Dots

On a blank piece of paper, one player draws five dots at random. The other player has to draw a character using the five dots: one as the head, two as the arms and two as the legs. A simple variation is to draw a zigzag which has to be incorporated into a drawing (but this time does not need to be of a person).

Redondo

This is a silly game that can make for a very entertaining afternoon of exuberantly creative though aimless drawing. The idea is not to produce recognisable forms, rather to be as abstract and free-form with your artwork as possible. Others then try to interpret your scribbles, and give the painting a caption.

Assemble a stack of scrap paper and as many types of drawing materials as you can muster. The idea is simply for people to draw, paint and daub to their heart's content. When a player is happy with his or her masterpiece, he shouts, 'Redondo!' and another player picks the artwork up, scrutinises it, lets its deep inner meaning infiltrate his or her soul and then writes an appropriate caption for the artwork. This captioned piece is then set aside on another pile.

After an agreed time limit is up or a certain number of artworks have been completed, the players take it in turns to display the work and read the captions. The assembled group's extraordinary creativity is put on exhibition.

Optical Illusions

The Wonder-Turner
(or, more exotically, the Thaumatrope)

This is really a Victorian marvel – described memorably by one author in the mid-nineteenth century as 'an exceedingly amusing toy, of very simple construction and pleasing effect'. You can't argue with that.

These are great fun to make and more fun can be had thinking of new subjects to paint or draw.

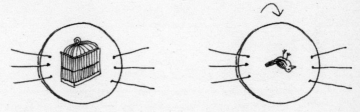

To make a simple Thaumatrope, cut out a circle of plain card – about 15cm or so in diameter. Use a darning needle or toothpick to make three small holes on either side of the disc, equally placed on and at either side of an imaginary diameter line (see diagram). Tie three bits of strong thread or string (each about 10cm long) through these holes as shown.

Now for the 'pleasing effect'. In a black pen, paint or draw a bird on one side of the disc and on the other side a cage. Make sure that the cage is upside down to the bird.

Now simply hold the centre strings on either side (quite close to the card) between the forefinger and thumb and twist the card rapidly around. The optical illusion produced is that of a bird in a cage.

Some other suggestions for images, depending on your artistic skill:

★ A juggler throwing up two balls on one side of a card, and two balls only on the other.
★ The body and legs of a man on one side, and his head and arms on the other.
★ A candle and its flame.
★ A mouse and a trap.
★ A horse and a rider.
★ A baby and cot.

Indoor Juggling

Juggling is one of those skills that is very satisfying to have, and once you've mastered the basics, you never lose the ability to do it. It's also maddeningly addictive once you get into it.

Start by practising with three beanbags or similar-sized fruit like large satsumas (before you invest in flaming torches, juggling pins and the like). Establish a place to practise – over a bed or a carpet is good – where the objects you'll be dropping will have a soft landing and won't bounce away. Also, if you stand with your knees against the side of a table or bed it prevents you from continually walking forward which can be a problem when you're practising your juggling.

The first step is to get the idea of what a good throw looks and feels like. Hold one of the beanbags in your right hand, cradled loosely in your fingertips; now throw it gently in an arc to your open left palm. The arc should peak at about eye level in front of you and ideally your hands should always be facing palm upwards and have to move very little to catch the bag. Repeat this step until you get the feeling and can catch the object in your left hand without looking.

Next put another beanbag in your left hand. Start again by throwing the bag from the right to the left hand but once it hits the top of the arc in front of your eyes, repeat the throw with your left hand aiming to get the second bag into your right hand. This is

when things start to get a bit messy and when the bed comes in handy. This will take a lot of practice – try to avoid the temptation to move your arms in a circle or to look at one of your hands. The bags will drop if you do this. Better to look straight ahead and try to keep the hands, arms and feet still.

When you've managed to complete one transfer, start again, and this time once the first beanbag hits the palm of your left hand, toss it back again towards your right so that both bags end up in the right hand. Once you've accomplished this you're ready to try to juggle the two bags continuously. Remember never to throw two bags at the same time.

And now you need to steel yourself for some frustration as you try to add the third beanbag into the mix. Start with two bags in your stronger hand, and once you have tossed the first bag, roll the second bag in that hand to the cradle of your fingertips and release it as the bag from the weaker hand hits 12 o'clock in its arc. Just try at first to do one round of three beanbags. Once you've succeeded, take a bow. Keep practising until you have a smooth transition while you're keeping these three objects in the air.

Now you can think about buying the flaming torches.

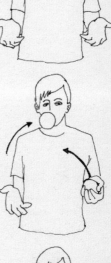

A Victorian Juggling Joke

Pick up two balls – one with each hand. Adopt a very serious face as if you are about to perform a complex and difficult trick. Stretch your arms out to their maximum width so that the balls are as far apart as they can be. Next lay down the challenge. Say that you will make both balls come into whichever hand your audience wishes without bringing the hands into contact with each other. When challenged to make this happen, all you have to do is to lay one of the balls down on a flat surface, turn around and take the ball up with the other hand.

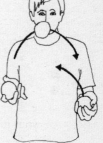

Memory Games

There are many kinds of memory games, but they can be broadly divided into visual and verbal challenges.

In verbal challenges, the task is usually to remember a list while adding an item of your own choosing for the next person to repeat. There are many variations of this kind of memory game, some of which are listed below. They have a nursery-rhyme quality to them, with players chanting the same refrain over and over, but also allow for some inventiveness and humour – you choose what the next person needs to remember so make it amusing!

Visual memory games involve recalling a set of objects which have been removed from view after a set period of contemplation. In Rudyard Kipling's *Kim*, the teenage protagonist is taught such a game in India, called the 'Play of the Jewels', as part of his rudimentary training to become a spy. His instructor, Mr Lurgan, spies on the Russians for the British, and runs a jewellery shop as cover. Lurgan brings out a copper tray and tosses a handful of jewels onto it; his boy servant explains to Kim, 'Look on them as long as thou wilt, stranger. Count and, if need be, handle. One look is enough for me. When thou hast counted and handled and art sure that thou canst remember them all, I cover them with this paper, and thou must tell over the tally to Lurgan Sahib. I will write mine.'

They play the game many times, sometimes with jewels, sometimes with odd objects, and sometimes with photographs of people. It is considered a vital part of training in observation; Lurgan says, '[Do] it many times over till it is done perfectly – for it is worth doing.'

In his book *Scouting Games* Robert Baden-Powell, the founder of the Scouts movement, then included what he called 'Kim's Game'. We've included it below, though you don't need to be a Scout, or Girl Guide, to play.

One problem with memory games, at least in the setting of children's parties, is that it is likely to be an adult who has to adjudicate, and the adult brain is rarely a match for the developing child's when it comes to retaining short-term memories. Be prepared for arguments!

VISUAL MEMORY GAMES

Kim's Game

One person, let's call them the traymaster, should collect on a tray a
number of articles – cutlery, playing cards, keys, pen, coins, jewellery,
and so on – no more than about fifteen items for the first few games
– and cover them over with a cloth. The other players all sit in view
of the tray and the traymaster then uncovers the objects for one
minute only. The players then have another minute to individually
list all the objects they can remember on a piece of paper. The
traymaster collects the lists and adds up how many objects each
player has correctly listed. Alternatively, players can swap papers and
mark each other.

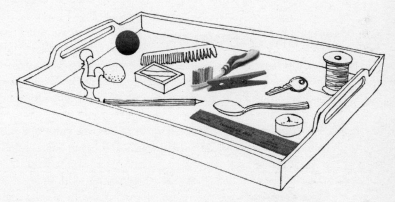

If everyone wants to play, then each player should take a turn at
being traymaster. Don't worry about having a completely different
set of objects for each round – it's actually more fun (and confusing)
if some of the objects reappear.

Variation: In this variation, the idea is not to remember what is on
the tray, but rather what has been removed.

Each turn a different item is removed from the tray of assorted
objects. Players must spot what is missing.

Feeling is Remembering

Fill a thick long sock with a number of objects. Make the selection
as diverse as possible – so think of lemons, keys, a box of matches, a
herb jar, a thimble, buttons. The sock is passed from one player to the
next and each has a minute to feel the different objects in the sock.

After the minute it is passed on to the next player while the first writes down as many objects as he or she identified and remembered. The winner is the person who has correctly identified and remembered the most objects.

What's Missing?

A room needs to be prepared before the guests arrive, by having some unusual objects added – the kitchen, living room and bathroom are all good. Allow the guests to have a good poke around for about five minutes and then send them out while you remove the unusual objects from the room. Now call them back in and give them a minute to write down everything they think is missing. The person who guesses the most is the winner.

VERBAL MEMORY GAMES

Some of these games, such as One Orange and A Good Fat Hen, have set rhymes, while others require players to make up a list of random objects which must be remembered by all players and in the correct order.

If you want to play these games strictly by the rules, and you have a large group of players, it might be as well to have one person making a list of the objects mentioned in the list, to avoid any squabbles.

One Orange

Players are seated in a circle. One player begins by saying, 'One orange,' to the player on his or her left. This is repeated around the circle. Now the first player repeats it, adding, 'Two terrible twins,' and the circle of players follows as before. As players forget the wording or sequence of the phrases, they drop out until a winner is left. The sequence goes:

> One orange
> Two terrible twins
> Three tender trusting teachers
> Four fat florid fussy fathers
> Five fearless fine flamboyant forgetful firemen
> Six slightly superior sisters singing sentimental songs
> Seven specially soulful seamen standing still staring seawards

A Good Fat Hen

This is a good game to play for forfeits. The group of players, which should be at least four but no more than ten, sits in a circle. The first person, player A, says, 'A good fat hen.' Each of the other players must repeat this until it gets to the last player, player B, who adds, 'Two ducks and a good fat hen.' Then this sentence is repeated until it reaches the last player before player B, who adds, 'Three squawking wild geese, two ducks and a good fat hen,' and so on. The list goes as follows:

A good fat hen
Two ducks
Three squawking wild geese
Four plump partridges
Five pouting pigeons
Six long-legged cranes
Seven green parrots
Eight screeching owls
Nine ugly turkey-buzzards
Ten bald eagles

So the last sentence, to be uttered by all, is, 'Ten bald eagles, nine ugly turkey-buzzards, eight screeching owls, seven green parrots, six long-legged cranes, five pouting pigeons, four plump partridges, three squawking wild geese, two ducks and a good fat hen.'

Any mistakes will result in a forfeit. This is a dangerous game to play in the pub.

John Ball

This is an entertaining variation of A Good Fat Hen.

First round – John Ball shot them all
Second round – John Block made the stock
Third round – John Brammer made the rammer
Fourth round – John Wyming made the priming
Fifth round – John Scott made the shot
Sixth round – John Crowder made the powder
Seventh round – John Puzzle made the muzzle
Eighth round – John Farrel made the barrel
Ninth round – John Clint made the flint
Tenth round – John Patch made the match

So, in the tenth round, each player has to say, 'John Patch made the match, John Clint made the flint, John Farrel made the barrel, John Puzzle made the muzzle, John Crowder made the powder, John Scott made the shot, John Wyming made the priming, John Brammer made the rammer, John Block made the stock, but John Ball shot them all.'

Good luck – really.

Hide and Seek Games

Hide and Seek

Probably one of the first games most children play and an endless source of entertainment around the house. For younger children, it's also a nice way to show off how well they can count.

The seeker closes his or her eyes, stands in a corner and counts to one hundred.

Meanwhile all others scatter to hide in different places in the house.

When the seeker nears a hundred, he or she shouts out, 'Ninety-eight, ninety-nine, one hundred! Here I come, ready or not!' and runs to find the hiders.

The first player to be found is the seeker in the next game.

Last to be found is the winner.

Sardines

A sort of reverse Hide and Seek.

Instead of there being one seeker, in Sardines there is only one hider who runs and finds a suitable space to hide in.

The rest of the players count up to a hundred and then disperse to find the sardine.

When a player finds the sardine, they join them in the hiding place. As more seekers find the sardines, the hiding place becomes very squashed – try to suppress giggles and shrieks or the hiding place becomes completely obvious to the remaining seekers.

Classic Board Games

While this book is not really about board games, and certainly not bored games, we couldn't pass the opportunity to remind everyone about these three classics, which were so much a part of life for previous generations, and which it would be lovely to think might be taken up by a few novices as a result of this book.

One delightful factor which they share is that you can play these games while quietly chatting amongst yourselves – they're a sociable challenge. Dominoes has long been associated with the pub – a half-pint on a corner table and a quick game – while draughts is an anytime, anywhere kind of contest. Tiddlywinks is a 'flat out on your stomach in front of the fire' activity, with a plate loaded with crumpets if you're lucky. Anyway, we hope you enjoy this refresher course in three all-time classics.

Draughts

Introduction to the Game of Draughts, published in 1756, was the first book in English to mention this compelling game. Dr Samuel Johnson wrote the preface and the dedication – he was a friend of the bookseller whose brother, William Payne, was the book's author. Writing in *The Life of Samuel Johnson*, James Boswell said, 'Johnson, I believe, did not play at draughts after leaving College, by which he suffered; for it would have afforded him an innocent soothing relief from the melancholy which distressed him so often … The game of draughts we know is peculiarly calculated to fix the attention without straining it. There is a composure and gravity in draughts which insensibly tranquillises the mind …'

What you need

There are a surprising number of variants to English Draughts (also known as American Checkers). The English draughts board has twelve counters for each side and the same layout as a chessboard – sixty-four alternating dark and light squares in a pattern of eight by eight (see illustration overleaf). But other versions of draughts have different configurations – Malaysian Checkers has a twelve-by-twelve board and thirty pieces per side, while Ghanaian Checkers has a ten-by-ten board and twenty counters per side!

Anyway, you'll need a board of sixty-four squares for English Draughts, which is the version we're concerned about here. You

could, of course, make your own square out of paper and colour in
the pattern. The counters are pretty easy to make too – twelve dark
and twelve light, though try to avoid having the same colours for
squares and counters as this can get confusing!

Aim of the Game

Draughts is a game for only two players. The aim, very simply, is to
take all of your opponent's counters, or leave your opponent with
nowhere to move.

How to Play

The counters should be set out in the pattern below, with the two
middle rows left empty. The row nearest each player is called the
king's row.

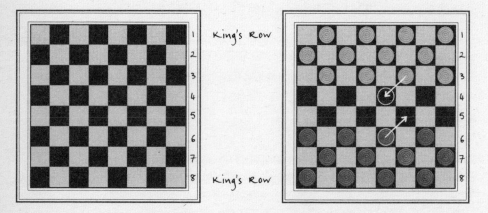

Kingʼs Row

Kingʼs Row

Moving

Players take it in turn to move their counters diagonally up the
board on the black squares, one square at a time, towards their
opponent. 'Kings' (see 'Crowning' below) can move forwards and
backwards but still only one square at a time and only on the black
squares.

Taking

When two pieces from different sides, let's call them white and black,
are moved by turn to adjoining squares, and the square behind one
of the pieces is empty, then the other must 'take' the counter by
'jumping' over into the empty square. The taken counter is then
removed from the board. A player MUST take a piece if they are in

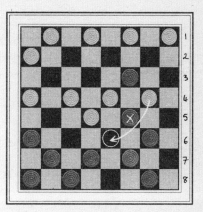

position to do so. And multiple pieces must
be taken in the same move if this is possible.
If there is more than one piece open to
attack, then the player must decide which
one to take.

In this illustration, white is taking a black
counter, but cannot take any pieces from the
next row as the squares behind them, in the
king's row, are occupied by black. Note that
black will have to take two of white's
counters in the next move, zigzagging over
the white counter in row six, and then the
centre right counter in row four.

Crowning

If a player's counter reaches the opponent's king's row, then that
counter is crowned and becomes a king. Reaching the king's row
and being crowned counts as one turn – the newly crowned king
can't move or capture a piece straight away, but must wait for the
next turn. Kings can be taken just like uncrowned pieces.

Winning

A player wins, as stated, by taking all of his or her opponent's pieces.

Tips for Winning: Early in the game, try to occupy the left of
centre square in row five if you are black, the right of centre square in
row four if you are white.

Also in the early stages of a game, try to protect yourself from
attack down the sides by moving a counter to the far left square in
row three, if you are black, or the far right square in row six if you
are white.

The first three moves are usually crucial to the outcome of the
game, but it's the endgame that matters most between accomplished
opponents. As you get better, try to win in the fewest possible moves.

Dominoes

This was one of Daisy's favourites. In the shop, after hours, she'd set
up the baize table and play Dominoes for hours. It was one of the
few games that would keep her full attention and the sound of the
clicking of the pieces against the silence of the night, and the rapt
concentration of the players, is one that sticks with us.

There's a lot of debate about where Dominoes originated – it seems that the Chinese had been playing tile-based games since about the twelfth century but the first appearance of Dominoes in Europe hasn't been traced back further than eighteenth-century Italy. There is no satisfactory etymology of the word 'domino' itself – it has been traced back to a word for a hooded cloak worn by priests but the connection with the tiles and game has never been convincingly explained.

What is clear though is that the game of Dominoes is a derivative of dice games. The tiles (or 'bones') with the two sets of dots (also called 'pips') on each end represent the throw of two dice. The blanks represent the throw of just one dice. These are all combined into a single set of twenty-eight bones which is the basis of the familiar game we play today.

Aim of the Game

The object of Dominoes is either to be the first to get rid of all of your bones or to block your opponent from making another move. The winner of a round of Dominoes gets an agreed number of points and the players play until one of them reaches a points target.

There are twenty-eight bones in a standard Dominoes set so the number of players will dictate how many dominoes each player has in his or her hand. If there are two or three players each player draws seven bones; if four or five then each player takes five. The pieces left over sit outside the game (called the 'boneyard'). The bones are generally placed upright balancing on the long edge of the tile, with the pips facing the player so that the other players cannot see their hand.

Game Play

The players draw their hands and whoever has double-six lays that first. If no one has double-six then the player who has double-five starts and, again, if that tile has not been picked by any player, then double-four is the starting tile and so on.

Once the game has started play moves in a clockwise direction around the table. Each player must try to match the number of pips on one half of a laid tile (the half that hasn't already been covered by another player's domino) with a tile from his hand. The two dominoes are placed end to end with the matching halves touching each other. Doubles are placed at right angles. So in the illustration below, the first move was double-six; the second player played six-five, the third six-three, the fourth five-five and so on. If a player cannot make a move, he has to miss a turn.

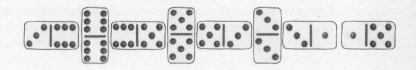

Winning the Game
The game proceeds until one player has played all his tiles or no other moves can be made. If the latter case, all players add up the number of pips on their remaining tiles with the player having the lowest total declared the winner.

Variation: A variation of this game requires a player who cannot make a move to take a new tile from the boneyard.

Tiddlywinks
Tiddlywinks has had a fairly lean time of it in the past few decades. In its boom time in the sixties the Goons, the most famous comedians of the day, battled it out with royalty (Prince Philip) and a team from Cambridge University in a game which became front-page news. Although it enjoyed its heyday then, the game had actually been invented in the 1880s but got its adrenalin shot of fame in the late 1950s when a group of students at Cambridge wanted to find a game at which they could represent their university. They settled on Tiddlywinks and within three years had started a varsity match against Oxford; by the end of the 1960s thirty-seven British universities had teams. Since then its popularity has waned somewhat but it is pretty easy to understand even if the purists will tell you that it takes a lifetime to master.

At its core the game requires you to use a 'Squidger' to propel a 'Wink' into a 'Pot'. Easy ... Well, maybe not.

The equipment consists of six winks (coloured plastic discs about 15mm diameter) of four different colours (blue, green, red and yellow), squidgers (diameter between 25mm and 51mm) which are the discs you press down on with your thumb to launch the winks, and a pot into which they are aimed.

In the modern game there are time limits and different varieties of game – the preferred is with two teams of two. Each player takes a colour (usually the blue and red team up) and there is a squidge-off in which whoever gets closest to the pot gains the right to start the game.

Players then take turns and try to score points or tiddlies, either by landing their winks in the pot or, more intriguingly, by attempting to squop their opponents' winks – that is, try to land on top of them.

If you get really good you can attempt boondocks (a move that shoots a wink off the mat or far from the main action), bristols (shots where the squidger is held perpendicular to the wink or winks), cruds (strong shots that separate winks in a pile) and John Lennon memorial shots (a shot which lands a wink on top of another wink) to win the game.

Aficionados claim that the game combines the physical dexterity of snooker with the strategic and mental prowess of chess and who are we to judge. In any case, we think it's worth a game for the pure silliness of the terminology alone.

Paper Modelling

Paper Aeroplanes

While we have all made paper aeroplanes at some point, very few travel beyond a disappointing nosedive on their maiden flight. There is an art to making a really reliable flyer, so here is a pretty foolproof set of instructions. Once you've mastered the basic model, there are plenty of variations and enhancements to experiment with.

1. Take a piece of A4 paper and fold it over vertically so that you have a strong crease running down the centre of the page.

2. Unfold the paper and fold the top corners into the centre of the page so that they touch each other along the fold you made in step 1.

3. Fold the top of the page (with the large triangle you just made back over itself), so that the top of the page is flat and the tip of the triangle is pointing towards the bottom of the page.

4. Fold the tip of the triangle back up again but not so that it is touching the top of the page. Leave a gap of about 1cm. (The gap helps lock the plane together when it flies.)

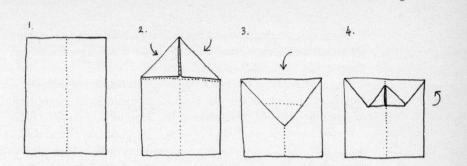

5. Take the top corners again and fold into the centre of the piece of paper as in step 2; this time unfold them so that you are left with a strong crease running from the top of the page to the side – the triangles don't need to align with the tip from step 4 but with the centre of the paper.

6. Using the folds you have just made as guides, bisect each of them with a fold tucking the paper behind the plane so that the plane has sloping shoulders. Unfold and you have two new creases.

7. Take the larger creases made in step 5 and fold inwards and towards you to the centre of the page.

8. Now fold along the crease made in step 6 (the larger of the two creases) and then tuck the bottom of each triangle under the flap created in step 4.

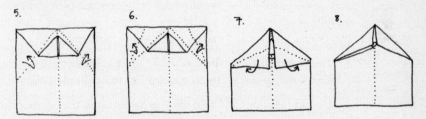

9. The 'plane' should now have a reasonably sturdy pyramid at the top. Fold down the middle again so that the side of the page with no folds showing is on top and the side with the folded-under parts is underneath. See diagram overleaf.

10. On both wings fold up in a straight line about 2cm from the edge of the page and then fold diagonally from the side of the aerofoil to the bottom of the paper to the width of the aerofoil.

When you lift the plane up these two small folds should point inwards to the middle of the plane and will help channel the air along the line of the plane. See final diagram.

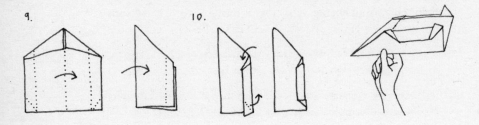

The world record for a paper aeroplane to spend 'time aloft' is 27.9 seconds. The record was set by Takua Toda in April 2009.

Paper Boats

Boats are easier to fold than planes – or at least this most basic model is. There are designs for catamarans and all sorts of complicated versions but this one works just as well.

1. Take a piece of A4 paper, fold it lengthways and open it up.

2. Fold it in half from top to bottom.

3. Fold the top corners into the middle of the page so that they meet snugly.

4. Take the bottom of the paper (there should be two loose flaps – work with one at a time) and fold the flap nearest you up horizontally so that it forms a neat line crease at the bottom of the two triangles. Turn the paper over and repeat this step. The paper should now have a triangle at the top and a solid bar running along the base.

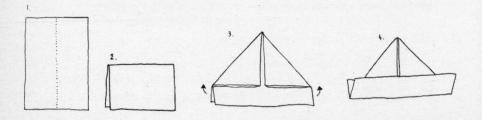

5. Push both thumbs up inside the main triangle and with the first fingers of both hands fold the end of the paper towards you, making a square with one corner facing down. The ends of the bar created in steps 3 and 4 can be tucked under one another.

6. Fold the bottom corner up so that it forms a triangle and turn the paper over and repeat on the other side.

7. Again push your thumbs up into the triangle and form a square so that there are two 'loose' triangles at the top of the paper.

8. Pull these two triangles carefully apart and you should create a vessel with a triangle sticking up in the middle which is the sail. Very simple.

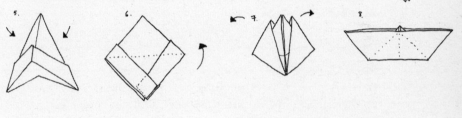

Now make lots with different colours of paper and sail them in a pond or in the bath!

Making an Origami Fortune Teller

We used to spend hours designing, making and playing with these. Once you've made your fortune teller the rules are pretty much up to you. First you need to make it.

1. Take a square of paper. Fold it in half, unfold it and then fold it in the opposite direction so that you have the paper with creases that show the square divided into quarters.

2. Next fold each corner precisely into the middle and make sure that the creases are quite strong.

3. Turn the sheet over and repeat that operation.

4. Turn the square over again and fold the square in half one way (creasing well), unfold and then fold again the other way. Now the fun begins …

5. Write a number on each segment from 1 to 8.

6. Open up each flap and write a fortune in each segment.

7. Turn the fortune teller over and write a colour on each of the 'pockets'.

8. Use your fingers to pick up the fortune teller.

To tell someone's fortune, get them to pick a colour from the colours written on the outside pockets. If they pick red, spell out r-e-d, while moving the fortune teller three times.

Now get the person to choose one of the numbers that are shown in the centre of the fortune teller when you have finished spelling out the colour. Let's say it is 3. You would move the fortune teller three times.

Then the person should choose a number from the ones showing this time. Whichever number they choose, lift up the flap and tell them their fortune.

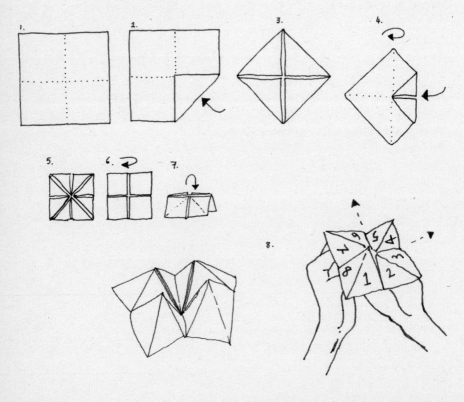

HALLOWEEN and BONFIRE NIGHT
Games and Pastimes

Halloween, or All Hallows Eve, is a celebration of the beginning
of winter and a time associated with ghosts and games. Along with
Bonfire Night on 5 November it's also a very welcome break from
the relentless, exhausting build-up to Christmas.

  Here are some of our favourite games, traditions and pastimes
associated with these festivals.

Halloween Games

Halloween has its origins back in pagan times, when it was a festival marking the time when the earth descended into a slumber (winter) to reawaken in spring. The Celts celebrated Halloween as a time when barriers between the living and the dead were weakened and spirits – good and bad – might make their way into our world. Costumes were sometimes worn to keep the evil spirits at bay and hence one of the traditions of Halloween began.

Apples have long been associated with this festival, as the fruit is harvested and stored at that time of year. Many Halloween games have arisen featuring apples.

Here's a good sequence of party games for children to play. Be warned – they're likely to get very messy and you might want to have some clean clothes, soap, water and towels on hand, and play in a room where cleaning up afterwards will be easy!

Bobbing for Apples (wet version)

You will need a large washing-up bowl or tub, enough apples – with stalks removed – so there is one for each player and plenty of towels for drying the players off afterwards.

There are several ways to approach this classic Halloween contest. The simplest is to fill a large washing-up bowl with water, add in some apples, and position all the players kneeling around the bowl with their hands behind their back. At a given signal, everyone tries to take an apple from the bowl using only their mouth. Make sure the bowl is big enough for all contestants to get around without banging heads! If you only have a small tub, you could make it a time trial using a watch or stopwatch to see how quickly each player can take an apple.

Alternatively, you could make the winner the first person to successfully take a bite out of an apple.

Other ways to make it a more difficult contest include blindfolding the players, and putting ice in the bowl with the apples – this can be numbing at Halloween but it certainly concentrates your efforts.

Bobbing for Apples (dry version)

An alternative version of Halloween apple bobbing which will leave your kitchen puddle free and not require a change of clothing! To play it you'll need an apple for each player, a skewer, some lengths of string or twine and a suitable, stable pole or beam to tie the apples to.

Make a vertical hole through each apple using a skewer, thread a piece of string or twine through each, then tie the strings onto something strong and stable – like a beam or pole, or even a tree branch. Make sure the apples are at easy biting heights! The players line up in front of the apples with their hands behind their backs and, at the signal, the first player to take a bite out of their apple is the winner.

Tip: To make the game harder, use bigger, firmer apples. To make it easier, smaller, softer apples are best.

Flour and Chocolate Game

After playing the watery version of Bobbing for Apples, go straight on to this game, and watch the wet faces become covered in a ghoulish, gooey white paste! You will need a big bag of flour, several packets of soft sweets – chocolate buttons are ideal – a large bowl and a plate.

Pour some flour into the bowl, then mix in a number of chocolate buttons or other suitable sweets. Next, add some more flour so that the bowl is completely filled. Pack the bowl tightly, patting it down with a wooden spoon. Now upend the bowl of flour on to a plate, so that it forms a mound on the plate like a sandcastle.

The wet-faced players take it in turns to try to find a sweet in the flour, again using only their mouths, with their hands behind their backs. After each player has had their turn, pat the flour down again. You could set up a cycle so that players have a go at bobbing for apples followed by this game immediately afterwards.

Bread and Treacle Game

Just to make sure the little monsters really do become little monsters, round off proceedings with this old family favourite!

Thickly spread some slices of bread or some scones with black treacle or chocolate spread, then tie a length of thread through each and attach them from the ceiling at a height that the players can reach with their mouths.

Now get the flour-faced ghouls to eat as many of the treacle titbits as possible. If you don't have a suitable beam or ceiling to attach the strings to, just stack the bread slices on a plate and get them to dive in (hands behind their backs of course).

Finally, two slightly less chaotic, but spirited games for Halloween parties.

Mad Scientist

This slightly gruesome Halloween game needs a little imagination and preparation in advance. It's sometimes known as Nelson's Eye and the game involves telling the children an eerie story about the Great Admiral Nelson and his embalmed body parts. In this version the story is that you are a Mad Scientist and you have just made a visit to the hospital laboratory!

The night before the party gather together a number of food items which you will pretend are various body parts, as follows:

★ Eyeballs – peeled, chilled grapes
★ Guts – warm noodles or spaghetti, tossed in oil
★ Hand – fill a rubber glove with water and freeze overnight, or fill with jelly and chill
★ Finger nails – toasted almond flakes
★ Ear – oyster mushroom
★ Tongue – small piece of raw chicken

Place all the body parts on a tray and cover with a cloth. Players are blindfolded as you take out each body part in turn to be passed around and touched as you tell the terrifying story of Nelson's remains or your Mad Scientist discoveries at the lab. Listen to the squeals of horror that ensue!

I Went to the Monsters' Ball ...

All you'll need for this are toffee apples or sweets for team prizes. It is a memory game designed to spook children just the right amount. It's also a good team game.

Get all the party guests sitting in a circle. The first child says, 'I went to the Monsters' Ball and I met Dracula and he went …!' They must then do a spirited impersonation of a vampire. The player sitting to the first player's left repeats the sentence and the action before adding, 'and then I met …' and introducing their own monster and impression. Carry on around the circle, with each player trying to remember the sequence of monsters and actions. If they can't, the other players must help until the circle has been completed. The team then share an appropriate prize – maybe some toffee apples?

Bonfire Night Traditions

Samuel Johnson defined 'Bonfire' in his Dictionary *(1755) as 'A fire made for triumph' and Bonfire Night was very much an exercise in triumphalism – celebrating the foiling of Guy Fawkes's plot to blow Parliament sky high.*

As a result of his treachery, Guy Fawkes came to be one of the most loathed (and burned) figures in English history, and on very early anniversaries celebrating his demise, disorder and extreme mayhem became so widespread that Bonfire Night had to be banned for a period before it could be revived in a more sedate form.

In Lewes in East Sussex, where some of the most extreme violence had taken place, the people created Bonfire Societies and marched together through the town carrying effigies before retiring to the outskirts to celebrate, each with their bonfire.

Over the centuries Bonfire Night became less politically heated and it is now celebrated as a late autumn tradition and an excuse to let off some fireworks – a highlight in the dark days and nights before Christmas – though the big festivals like that at Lewes still have a fairly primeval feel to them.

There are many customs associated with the night – gathering wood for the fire, making a 'Guy' and collecting money to buy fireworks, chanting rhymes and making particular kinds of seasonal treats like toffee apples and parkin cake.

Toffee Apples

Ingredients
8 crisp apples
400g golden caster sugar
1 tsp wine vinegar
4 tbsp golden syrup
100ml water

Cover the apples with boiling water in a large bowl. (This helps remove the waxy coating and makes the toffee stick better.) Take the stalks off, dry the apples and push a lollipop stick (chopsticks or wooden skewers also work well) into the bottom of each apple.

Heat the sugar in a heavy pan with 100ml of water and cook over a medium heat until the sugar dissolves (about five minutes) then add the vinegar and syrup. Use a sugar thermometer to bring the liquid to 140°C. (If you don't have a sugar thermometer, you can always check by simply taking some of the mixture and dropping it into a bowl of cold water. If the toffee sets immediately and is brittle when it is taken out, it is ready.)

Dip the apples in the toffee to completely coat them. Place them, lollipop stick up, on a layer of greased baking paper and allow to cool and set.

SOME BONFIRE NIGHT RHYMES

Remember, remember, the fifth of November
Gunpowder, treason and plot!
I see no reason, why gunpowder treason
Should ever be forgot.

Guy Fawkes, Guy, t'was His intent
To blow up king and parliament.
Three score barrels were laid below
To prove old England's overthrow.

By God's mercy he was catch'd
With a darkened lantern and burning match.
So, holler boys, holler boys, let the bells ring.
Holler boys, holler boys, God save the king.

And what shall we do with him?
Burn him!

Remember, remember, the fifth of November,
Gunpowder, treason and plot!
A stick or a stake for King James's sake
Will you please to give us a faggot
If you can't give us one, we'll take two;
The better for us and the worse for you!

Guy Fawkes, Guy,
Stick him up on high,
Hang him on a lamp post
And there let him die.
Guy, Guy, Guy,
Poke him in the eye,
Put him on the fire
And there let him die.
Burn his body from his head,
Then you'll say
Guy Fawkes is dead.
Hip, hip, hooray!

Rumour, rumour, pump and derry,
Prick his heart and burn his body,
And send his soul to Purgatory.

WINTER EVENINGS

As the nights draw in and going outside seems uninviting by five
o'clock in the evening, these classic card and dice games will provide
hours of entertainment. They are all pretty straightforward to play,
and there are lots of games here for all the family.

Card Games

'One should always play fairly when one has the winning cards.'

Oscar Wilde

With their origins in four continents and a history that stretches back well over a thousand years, playing cards have been a source of pleasure ever since man invented the chair to sit back on and the concept of shared entertainment of a competitive but friendly sort (of course, it's not always that friendly, and family games can be deadly).

The beauty of cards is that they can be played almost anywhere at any time. They can be played alone, meditatively, or in a raucous evening of gambling and laughter.

There are literally hundreds of card games. Our choice aims to give you a selection of games to suit every occasion so that there is something here for all the family – young and old. There are some interesting patience challenges, some games which suit two players and many which are better with a larger group – usually four players and upwards.

We've also gone for games which don't require any special equipment, nothing more complicated than packs of cards, pens, paper and some form of gambling currency – be it money, chips or chocolate, or whatever takes your fancy.

Playing cards arrived in Europe in the fourteenth century by which time the four suits and ranks of cards were already established. The first packs of cards were handcrafted and only affordable to the aristocracy. It wasn't until the next century that packs were made more widely available through advances in printing.

The designs we know and love today, with the familiar suits and court cards, probably originated in France. One of the first mentions of playing cards in Britain is in an Act of Parliament in 1463, banning imports of foreign cards. Since then they've had a chequered history in these isles, being regarded as either the scourge of society or the very last thing in sophistication.

In a pamphlet published around the time of the English Civil War, cards were used as a symbol of the decadence of King Charles I. The conflict was metaphorically described as a 'Bloody Game of Cards, played between the King of Hearts and his Suite against the rest of the pack, shuffled at London, cut at Westminster, dealt at York, and played in the open field'.

In the next century, a writer about cards and other pastimes in the 1750s observed that, 'Gaming is become so much the Fashion amongst the Beau-Monde, that he who, in company, would appear ignorant of the Games in Vogue, would be reckoned low-bred, and hardly fit for Conversation.'

A hundred years later, in Lewis Carroll's 1865 classic, *Alice's Adventures in Wonderland*, many of the characters are playing cards. Carroll made Alice's main adversary the Queen of Hearts, whose cry of 'Off with their heads!' rings through the pages of the book. The cards were a perfect cipher for Alice's struggle to negotiate the path from childhood to adulthood, representing as they do elements of both worlds – play, gambling, chance, logic and order. Carroll said that he 'pictured … the Queen of Hearts as a sort of embodiment of ungovernable passion – a blind and aimless Fury'.

In the early twentieth century a different social class – British soldiers in the trenches of the First World War – developed a passion for the French card game, *Vingt-et-un* (Twenty-one), which they brought back to Britain as Pontoon. It's a game that can be played quickly and by large groups of people, which no doubt partly accounted for its popularity in the grim surroundings of the battlefield.

With the dawn of the TV age and mass communication, cards lost some of their ubiquity, but they continue to inspire and entertain new generations, even if many people's first experience of card games is now on the internet.

For all the following card games, the jokers should be removed from the pack before playing.

CARD GAMES FOR ONE PLAYER

Single-player card games, known as patience or solitaire, are great for solitary moments or for when you need to take your mind off the concerns of everyday life.

Most patience games take only a little time to play, though winning becomes an addiction. They generally require some good luck and judgement to play out – you are at the mercy of the shuffled deck, after all – but not so much that your mind can't sift through other thoughts.

For children patience is a great introduction to the basic mathematics and routines that most card games contain, and for adults it's a reminder that the simple deck of cards can be as enjoyable a diversion as any computer game or TV programme.

Elevens

Cards
One full pack of fifty-two cards. Aces count as one; the picture cards (jack, queen, king) can only be played as a three-card sequence.

Aim of the Game
To play out the full pack by pairing up and covering cards that have a combined numerical value of eleven.

How to Play
Deal nine cards, face up in a rectangle of three rows by three columns. If any two cards appear which add together to give a numerical value of eleven (10 and ace, 9 and 2, 8 and 3, 7 and 4, 6 and 5, and so on), cover each of the cards in this pair with a fresh card from the pack.

This will then (hopefully!) provide another or more pairs to be covered.

Any picture cards must be left uncovered until there are no non-picture cards which can be paired up. (This may, of course, be the situation when you have dealt the initial nine cards, in which case collect and shuffle the pack and start again.) If, and only if, at this point you have a jack, a queen AND a king in the grid of nine cards, these are then covered in the sequence – jack, queen, king. (Only one or two of the picture cards is not enough!) If the cards you cover the royal cards with produce more combinations of eleven, carry on playing to play the pack out.

If not, you must collect and shuffle the pack and begin again.

If you do manage to play the pack out, it's a great method of shuffling the cards.

Auld Lang Syne

This is another game which is easy to play in a restricted space. It's quite a tricky one to 'win' as well, as you watch the cards you need disappearing down the growing piles. The chances of building four complete piles have been estimated to be about one in a hundred but you may consider this optimistic after an hour of playing. Still, it's good fun.

Cards

One full pack of fifty-two cards.

Aim of the Game

To build four complete piles of consecutively ranked cards, from ace (low) to king (high), regardless of suit.

How to Play

The four aces are separated from the pack and laid face up in a row as four bases, to which the player will hope to add cards in their numerical sequence but disregarding suits.

Four cards are then dealt face up in a row directly beneath the aces. If one of the cards is a 2, it can be placed on one of the aces, and the beginning of a sequence is built. If there is a 3 present, this can, in turn, be placed on the 2. Once all the four cards have been added to the bases, and there may be none of course, the player deals another four cards, filling any gaps and covering the remaining cards. You must lay down all four new cards before making any possible moves.

Play continues like this until the entire pack has been dealt out, at which point there will either be four piles of ace to king, or the player will have failed, as sequences become 'blocked', and will have to start again – there is no redealing of the pack.

Flower Garden

Cards

One full pack of fifty-two cards.

Aim of the Game

To build four complete 'foundation' piles of the suits, from ace (low) through to king (high).

How to Play

Deal out six columns of six overlapping cards face up, and place the remaining sixteen cards in a fan around the top of the columns. The columns are the 'flower beds' and the fanned-out cards are the 'seedlings'.

The bottom card of each of the flower beds, and any of the seedling cards, can be moved according to the rules. The other cards in the flower beds must be uncovered before they can be moved.

To start with, any aces exposed at the bottom of the flower beds, or in the row of seedlings, should be placed in a row above or below the flower bed – wherever there is space – to make the foundation beds of hearts, clubs, diamonds and spades. The aim of Flower Garden, like many patience games, is to build up these suits in order, from ace to king.

So any exposed 2s and then 3s might also be added to their respective aces on the foundation piles. Now it gets trickier, as you have to work to uncover further cards. In a good hand the aces and 2s will be close to the bottom of the flower beds, or in the row of seedlings. In a bad one, they will be further up the flower beds and difficult to get to.

Cards may be moved from the bottom of one bed, or the seedling row, to another as long as they are placed at the bottom of the bed, on a card which is of immediately higher rank – suits don't matter. So the 3 of diamonds might be placed on the 4 of spades, or the queen of hearts on the king of hearts. This will expose cards which might be placed on the foundation piles, or moved to yet another bed to expose another card. Cards cannot be moved from the flower beds or foundation piles to the seedling row. Cards can only be moved one at a time – no sequences of cards can be moved together as they can in other forms of patience.

When a flower bed becomes vacant, because all the cards have been moved to the foundation piles or other beds, any card from the bottom of the other beds, or the seedling row, may be moved to the space to renew the bed.

Try to avoid moving cards from the seedling row to the flower beds, if you can, as the cards in the bed will be even further buried in the pile.

Variation: To make the game easier, cards can be moved in sequences, so if you have built up a set of 7, 6, 5 in one column, you can move it to another (provided it is moved onto an 8, of course). The cards do not have to be in the same suit.

King Albert

This is a tricky game of patience – all the cards are dealt face up making them seem tantalisingly available, but winning the game is not so easy.

Cards

A full pack of fifty-two cards.

Aim of the Game

To build four complete 'foundation' piles of the suits, from ace (low) through to king (high).

How to Play

Deal out all but seven of the cards in rows, face up. The first row is nine cards, the second row is dealt over the first eight cards of the first row, overlapping them face up. The third row is dealt over the first seven cards of the second row and so on, until you finish with a card on the end of the first column, again face up.

The seven remaining cards are placed face up in a reserve row, side by side. Space should be left for the four foundation piles which will (hopefully) be built from the four aces upwards. During the game, cards can only be moved one at a time, from the exposed bottom of the columns or the reserve pile. No sequences of cards can be moved.

To start with, any exposed aces should be moved to form the foundation piles, and then any 2s or 3s of the corresponding suits which are similarly free to grab. Now comes the luck and judgement part. Cards can be moved onto other columns as long as the card they overlap is a different colour (e.g. hearts onto clubs, spades onto

diamonds). This is with the aim of exposing the cards beneath them which can be moved onto their suit's foundation pile, in ascending sequence. Cards can be played from the reserve pile as long as they conform to the same rules. So, if you have the ace of diamonds on a foundation pile, you might move the 3 of diamonds onto the 4 of clubs, to expose the 2 of diamonds. The 2 of diamonds can then be moved onto the ace and followed by the 3 of diamonds. Finally if you clear a column you can fill it with any exposed card. Sounds more complicated than it is. Once you put the cards down it all becomes clear. Not necessarily easy, though.

CARD GAMES FOR TWO OR MORE PLAYERS

Pairs (also called Pelmanism)

Cards
A full pack of fifty-two cards.

Aim of the Game
To match and collect the greatest number of pairs.

How to Play

Shuffle the pack and lay all the cards face down on a table, making sure none of the cards are touching. One player starts by turning over two cards from anywhere on the table, in full view of everyone. If they are a matching pair (e.g. Two jacks, two 9s etc.) then he or she removes them and places them face down in a personal pile.

If they don't match, the cards should be quickly and carefully turned over again, and the next player takes their turn. As the game progresses, players must attempt to remember the location of cards, so they can match pairs and build up their stack. The winner is the player with the most pairs once no cards remain on the table.

Draw the World Dry

A lot of people call this Strip Jack Naked or Draw the Well Dry. We can't be sure when we misheard it but for us it has always been Draw the World Dry. It could be because it felt so interminable to our parents.

Cards

A full pack of fifty-two cards.

Aim of the Game

For one player to win all the cards in the pack.

How to Play

Choose a dealer who shuffles and deals all the cards out face down. It doesn't matter if you end up with a slightly uneven distribution. The hands should be stacked in a pile in front of each player.

The player to the left of the dealer now plays a card from the top of his or her stack into the middle of the table. Then the player to the left again does the same, covering the card on the table so that a pile starts to form.

As soon as someone turns up one of the picture cards or an ace, the next player has to cover it with the following number of cards:

Jack – one card
Queen – two cards
King – three cards
Ace – four cards

If he or she plays the required number of cards without turning up a picture card or an ace, then the player who originally played the picture card takes the whole pile from the table and places them face down at the bottom of his or her pile. This player then plays the next card and the game continues.

If, however, a picture card or ace is turned up before the specified number of cards, then the player next to him or her must start the process again, laying four cards for an ace, three for a king etc.

A player who runs out of cards is out of the game, even if he or she runs out of cards while responding to a picture card, in which case the player who laid it takes the pack as usual. Eventually someone will end up with all the cards. A word of warning – sometimes this can take a long time.

Old Maid

Players
Two to five players. This is a really simple game to learn, making it suitable for children of all ages, as the saying goes.

Cards
A full pack of fifty-two cards with one of the queen cards taken out, other than the queen of spades.

Aim of the Game
The player left holding the 'Old Maid' – the queen of spades – is the loser.

How to Play
The cards are dealt out among the players – it doesn't matter if one or two hands contain the odd card more. Each player goes through his or her hand and removes any cards paired by rank which are discarded on a pile in the middle. (Any pairs of 2s or 5s, for example.)

Each player in turn then shuffles his or her hand briefly and offers it, face down in a fan, to the player to the left who must choose one card. If this card can be paired with one from this player's own hand, he or she may discard both cards in the middle. If not, it must be kept, briefly shuffled and then offered to the player on his or her left. This goes on until only the Old Maid is left.

This is another game that benefits from being played quickly, with the Old Maid hopefully changing hands frequently.

Slap-Jack

A game requiring quick reactions rather than quick wits, this is loved
by all age groups. Watch out for squabbles among less experienced
card players, or those at the end of a long evening.

Cards

One full pack of fifty-two cards for up to six players. For more players,
two full packs is advisable.

Aim of the Game

To collect all the cards in the pack, by being the first to claim jacks.

How to Play

Deal the full pack out clockwise and face down in piles in front of
the players – don't worry if the distribution is uneven. The player to
the dealer's left takes the top card from his or her pile and places it in
the centre of the table – this is the discard pile. The card must only
be turned over when it is immediately above the discard pile – no
player, including the one holding the card, should see what it is until
it is placed. This is very important.

The player to this person's left does the same and so on, until
someone turns over a jack. At this point all the players must compete
to slap their hand on the jack. The first one to do so wins the pile,
which is added to the bottom of his or her own pile with the jack
turned face down. This player then begins the next round.

If a player 'slaps the jack' incorrectly – on a king or a queen, for
instance – then the top card of this player's pile must be given to the
player of the card. The more fastidious players might insist that the
winning pile is shuffled, but we think trying to remember when a
jack might next appear adds to the fun.

A player who loses all his or her cards has one last chance to slap
the next jack before being finally out of the contest.

Play continues until one player has gained all the cards and is
therefore the winner.

Nap

Nap, short for 'Napoleon', is another great game for family evenings,
combining simplicity of play with tense and skilful gambling. It has
been a popular game in Britain for well over two hundred years.

Players

Two to eight. The fewer the players, the more luck there is involved in winning, because a greater proportion of the cards are 'sleeping' – unused in the deck.

Cards

A full pack of fifty-two cards, with aces ranking high and 2 being the low card.

Aim of the Game

To bid a number of tricks to win, and then accumulate chips or money by achieving that bid.

How to Play

The dealer, once decided, deals each player five cards, face down. The remaining cards are placed in a pile in the centre of the table.

The player to the dealer's left then starts the bidding. Looking at his or her cards, this player assesses how many of the five rounds, or tricks, he or she is likely to win, and declares that to the other players. If the next player thinks they can do better, then they can bid a higher number. If someone bids to win all five tricks, they are bidding a Nap (Napoleon) hand. If this bid is made, and only after it is made, it can be topped by someone else calling 'Wellington'. This is the same as a Nap bid – all five tricks – but paying out more if defeated. The minimum bid is two tricks, although players don't have to bid – if they think their hand is poor they can pass.

The player with the highest bid then lays his or her first card – this suit automatically becomes trumps. The others, going round from this player's left, must then play a trump card or discard one from a different suit. If the bidding player wins the hand, he or she has won one of his bid tricks and continues. If the hand is lost, then he or she must try to win back the lead, and carry on to win the bid. Of course if the player has bid 'three' he must endeavour to lose two of the five tricks as well as winning his three.

If he is successful, the bidding player takes from each player the same number of coins or chips as he has bid or, if he loses, he must pay that amount (two chips for a bid of two etc.). If he has bid Nap, then he gets ten chips from each player, but must only pay five if he fails. For a bid of Wellington, he must be paid ten if he wins, but also pay ten if he loses.

The game can continue until one player has won all the chips, or until a prearranged number of hands has been played, at which point players may count their stack of winnings to see who has been victorious.

Daisy's Game

Our grandmother was a Nap fiend – most evenings over the Christmas holidays were devoted to Nap schools and we would play long into the night, listening to her catalogue of advice and sayings as she slowly wiped out our piles of matchsticks.

In this variation named in her honour, the player bidding Nap may look at the top card in the leftover pile, and exchange it for a card in her hand, if she thinks it will improve it. With a Wellington bid, the player must stick with her own cards – not having a peek at the top card.

Daisy Sayings
'He's coming off windy' – Player is chancing his arm.
'Keep a red 'un' – Default advice when faced with a tough decision.
'He's playing like Dicky's hat band' – We never got to the bottom of what this actually meant. The general sense was that the player with the highest bid had a dodgy hand.

Tip: When trying to defeat a player who has bid Nap, it is usually more effective to keep a pair of a suit until last rather than two high cards from different suits.

Rummy

Players
Two to six players.

Cards
A full pack of fifty-two cards – kings are high and aces are low. You will also need a pen and paper for scoring.

Aim of the Game
To avoid accumulating points by playing all your cards to the table in sets or 'melds'.

How to Play
The dealer deals one card at a time face down, clockwise. Two players receive ten cards each, three or four players get seven cards,

and five or six players are dealt six cards each. The remaining pack is placed in a pile face down in the middle of the table, and the top card is turned up beside it to form a discard pile.

Going clockwise from the dealer's left, each player can either replace a card from their hand with the visible top card on the discard pile, or take a card unseen from the top of the remaining pack, which they may choose to exchange with one of their hand or to discard.

Between taking a card and discarding one, the player may lay down sets of three or four cards of the same rank, or three or more cards of the same suit in sequence. Each set is known as a meld. At the same time, they may add cards to the melds they already have – a 7 to three 7s, for instance, or the ace and 2 of clubs to the 3, 4, 5 and 6 of clubs. This player may also add cards to other players' melds.

The play continues clockwise around the table until one player 'goes out' – either by discarding as normal or by melding and laying down all the cards in their hand in one instance – called 'going Rummy'. This is an effective tactic if you don't want your opponents to know that you are close to going out, and also costs your opponents more points. Once a player has ended the game in either way, the other players must keep all their cards for scoring.

Each losing player must calculate the number of points they have accumulated in that hand, with picture cards counting ten points, aces one point, and the other ranks according to their numerical value. The score is doubled if a player has successfully gone Rummy. The total number of points is their score for that hand, and the winner is the player with the lowest score when someone passes the hundred points mark, or the two hundred mark. It's such an addictive game that you won't be surprised to hear yourself saying, 'Shall we play to five hundred?'

CARD GAMES FOR THREE OR MORE PLAYERS

Newmarket

Although ostensibly named after the famous racecourse, Newmarket has many other names and has been a family favourite for years. Anyone who has played as a child will remember the ghastly tension of watching a round being played out, where you didn't have a backed 'horse', waiting for someone to claim the pile of pennies on the jack

of clubs, or king of diamonds, and worse, the bulging central kitty of
pennies. These are the kinds of experiences that either put you off
gambling for life or ensure the continued survival of Ladbroke's.

Players
Three to eight players.

Aim of the Game
To win money on the horses and also win the kitty by disposing of
all your cards during play.

Cards
One full pack of fifty-two cards, a 10 of spades, jack of clubs, queen
of hearts and king of diamonds from another pack – these four cards
are the horses which the players bet on. Kings are high and aces low.

How to Play
Divide the money or chips you're going to play with equally amongst
the players. Place the kitty pot, or plate, in the middle of the table and
place the four horses around it in a square. Decide who is going to be
the dealer. The deal will subsequently go to the left.

Before the deal, each player should place a bet on the horse, or
horses, of their choice – four coins or chips – and another coin into
the kitty. The pack of cards is now dealt out one at a time face down
to each of the players and also one card to a dummy or 'dead' hand.
It may be, depending on numbers, that some players receive more
cards than others – don't worry, this will even itself out over the
course of the game. Once the deal is done, players may, if they wish,
bid to buy the dead hand to replace their own, the proceeds going
in the kitty. They might do this if their hand contains no horses,
for instance.

The player to the left of the dealer must now lay in front of them
the lowest card in a suit of their choice, announcing the name of the
card as they do so. This player, for instance, may say, 'The ace of
spades,' or 'The three of diamonds' – as long as they pick the lowest
card they have in whichever suit they prefer. (It's quite likely that, if
the player has a horse, they will pick that suit!) The player who holds
the next highest card in that suit must now play it, and so on.

When either the king of that suit is reached, or the sequence comes
to an end because the next card is contained in the dead hand, the last
player to lay down must start a new sequence by laying the lowest
card in their hand, again in the suit of their choosing. This may be the

same suit as before, and it may be a lower card than the previous sequence started in. So, for instance, the first player may have started a sequence with the 3 of diamonds (their lowest diamond). The second player may have ended the sequence with the 9 of diamonds (the 10 of diamonds being in the dead hand). They may then choose to play the 2 of diamonds, as their lowest card in that suit, just to get rid of it and retain the lead.

If a sequence continues until one of the players lays down and announces one of the horses, that player then collects the money which has been bet and placed on that card. The sequence must be continued after this, if there are any more cards in play. So, if a player takes their winnings from the queen of hearts, and another player has the king of hearts, then it must be laid down to end the sequence of hearts.

Play goes on until one player lays down their final card, ending the round. This player also wins the kitty for that hand. If any of the horses have unclaimed bets on them at the end of the round, the money or chips can either be left to accumulate, or placed in the kitty to boost it – whichever approach is to be taken should be decided in advance. It can be quite nail-biting to watch a sequence end before it reaches the horse you have held in your hand!

The player to the left of the original dealer now takes their place, the player to this new dealer's left lays the first card, and so on. The game continues until one player has won all the money, or until a prearranged time. Proceedings can be wound down by turning over the horses, one at a time, so there are fewer choices to bet on and the stake on each card increases.

Pontoon

This is the British equivalent of Blackjack – the big casino game – and is thought to have been brought back here from the First World War trenches in France where it was popular with the soldiers.

There are so many variations and rules for Pontoon that it would be impossible to cover them all here, so we've included a simplified version that can be easily picked up by everyone. It's not a complicated game anyway.

Cards

One full pack of fifty-two cards, with picture cards counting ten, aces one or eleven, and the remaining cards holding their own numerical value. You will also need money, chips or their equivalent – matchsticks are always good. Agree minimum and maximum stakes for each round to avoid arguments later.

Players
Three to ten.

Aim of the Game
To beat the banker on each hand by getting the closest score to twenty-one points – pontoon. Each player is competing only against the banker on each round, rather than against the other players.

How to Play
The first player to be dealt a jack becomes the banker, who deals each player, including himself, one card face down. All players except the banker look at their card and decide how much they want to bet, placing this amount beside their face-down card.

The banker then deals all the players a second card which, again, they may look at but he or she may not. Finally, the banker goes around the table, starting with the person to the left, giving each player three options:

★ They can 'stick' with the hand they have, and take no more cards from the bank. A player cannot stick if their hand totals less than sixteen.

★ They can 'buy' a card face down from the bank, in which case they must add to their original bet with a sum not exceeding it. So if the original bet was three matches, then they could pay one, two or three matches for a third card, depending on how they want to gamble and their judgement of the hand. Further cards can be bought face down, to a maximum total number of five cards in the hand. For each card bought, the rule applies that the amount the player bets cannot exceed the sum paid for the previous card.

★ The player can 'twist' – receive a card face up. This card, and subsequent twists, are free, but the player cannot buy a card once he or she has twisted. The player's original two cards should remain face down, so the banker does not know their worth.

A player who gets to a total of twenty-one at any stage must stop, as this is the maximum score allowed. Anyone who gets over twenty-one goes 'bust', and must hand his or her bet and cards to the banker, who puts the cards to the bottom of the pack and keeps the stake!

When the banker has dealt with all the players, he must try to equal or better the hands remaining in the game – which haven't gone bust. The banker turns over his two cards and plays the game as the other players have done before until he decides to stick, goes bust or achieves a higher total than the other players. He either takes money off players if he has beaten them or pays the players the amount they have staked during the course of the hand.

If a player gets a pontoon (a picture card and an ace) then, unless the bank is also dealt the same hand, that player takes over ownership of the bank.

Cheat

Players
Three to eight – more than four is more fun. While this can be great fun for adults in the right frame of mind, it is primarily a children's game; indeed, it is often their first experience of playing cards.

Cards
One full pack of fifty-two cards for three or four players. Two full packs, shuffled together, for more than four players. Aces are high.

Aim of the Game
To be the first player to get rid of all the cards in their hand.

How to Play
All the cards are dealt out, one at a time and face down. The player to the left of the dealer plays up to four cards face down, in the middle of the table, saying what they are: 'Three 7s', for example. The next player must then play their cards (up to eight if there are more than four players and you are playing with two packs). This player must also declare their cards and they must be in the rank immediately above or below the previous player's cards. So they might say, in this example, 'Four 8s,' or 'Two 6s.' If the rank is aces, the next call can be either kings or 2s.

Of course, both players may be lying to varying degrees – they may have one 7, two 8s or no 6s – that's why the game is called Cheat. If another player suspects that their opponent has lied about the cards she has laid, then they can shout, 'Cheat!' and the game stops. The number of cards that the player claimed to have put on the pack are taken and placed face up. If they are lying, they must take all the cards in the pile and their accuser begins the next round. If, however, they are telling the truth, and really did have four aces, or three 7s, then they start the next round after their accuser has added the pile of cards to their hand.

The first player to get rid of all their cards is the winner. This is a game best played quickly.

Variation: Players can lay one card down at a time, if you want the game to continue for considerably longer. You might want to see how you go with the proper game first.

Ranter Go Round

This old game, another one for the children to enjoy, is thought to have originated in Cornwall, though it is also known as Cuckoo, which was played in Europe in the seventeenth century. It is a good game to play when time is tight as the rounds go quickly.

Players
This can be played by three players but also by twenty or more.

Cards
One full pack of fifty-two cards. Kings are high and aces are low. You will also need some counters – coins or matchsticks, or even chocolates will do, if you can trust yourself.

Aim of the Game
Each player gets three lives. The winner is the last person left in when all the other players have used up their lives.

How to Play
The dealer gives each player one card, face down. The lowest card at the end of the round will be the losing hand. The player to the dealer's left looks at his or her card and decides whether exchanging cards with the person to his left is likely to achieve a higher rank. If he thinks he will, he says, 'Change,' and they must exchange cards. If he thinks he should keep his card, he says, 'Stick.'

The only exception is when a player has a king, the highest card, in which case he or she should place this face up in front of him at the beginning of the round. The player to the right cannot exchange his card on this hand.

The round continues until finally it is the turn of the dealer who may exchange his card for the top one from the pack, if so wished.

The cards are then revealed, and the player with the lowest card loses a counter, or life. If there are two people with the same lowest card, they both lose a life.

The player to the left of the dealer now deals the next round, and play continues, with players dropping out when they have lost their three lives, until only one remains – the winner.

Hearts

This is another very simple but very exciting game to play, which can be mastered and enjoyed by children older than eight.

Players
Three to six with four being the optimum number.

Cards
The full pack of fifty-two cards is used for four players. For three players, the 2 of clubs is removed, for five players the 2 of clubs and the 2 of diamonds are removed, and for six players the 2 of clubs, the 2 of diamonds, the 2 of spades and the 3 of clubs are omitted.

Aim of the Game
To avoid taking tricks containing hearts, which each count as one point, and thus end up with the lowest score when one player ends the game by accumulating fifty or more points. However, if a player can take all the tricks with hearts in them, then that player may deduct thirteen points from their score.

How to Play
The dealer deals the pack out clockwise, face down, one card at a time – all hands should contain the same number of cards, with cards removed according to the number of players as described above.

The player to the left of the dealer leads with the card of their choice and the other players must follow suit if they can, or discard from another suit. There are no trumps – the highest card played wins the trick, and the player who wins must then place the trick in front of them and take the lead. Hearts can be played when the player can't follow suit.

All the tricks are played out until the cards have been used up, and then all the players add up how many points (hearts) they have accumulated and a note is made.

If a player has a hand containing a number of higher-ranking hearts – or possibly a hand where they feel they can win all the tricks anyway – then they might 'go for the lot'. They should keep this quiet so players don't arrange their hands to stop them from the outset. If they succeed, then, as stated above, that player can deduct thirteen points from their score. If unsuccessful, then the tally of hearts gets added to their total as usual.

Black Lady

This variation really beefs up the tension in a game of Hearts, and as a result is as well known as the game it derives from. The Black Lady is the queen of spades, and adds thirteen points to the score of the player who takes it in a trick. This is as many points as all the hearts together, and so is to be avoided as far as possible.

We used to play endless games of this after dinner – sometimes passing the queen of spades to someone you're feuding with does manage to alleviate family tensions!

Players

Three to six players are best.

Cards

The full pack of fifty-two cards, distributed as for Hearts (above).

The Aim of the Game

Either dispose of the Black Lady and all your hearts cards, keeping your score as low as possible until another player reaches a tally of fifty or one hundred points (to be agreed). Or 'go for the lot' if you think you can capture *all* the hearts cards and the queen of spades. In this scenario, if you're successful, twenty-six points are wiped from your score.

How to Play

The procedure is similar to Hearts but with some essential changes. Once the cards have been dealt, each player must choose three cards from his or her hand which are then passed to the player to the right, and receive three from his or her own left in turn.

Unless you are going for the lot, it makes sense to dispense with the king and ace of spades, if you have them without the queen, and similarly high hearts, as you're more likely to 'win' tricks with these cards and attract the Black Lady!

Another rule peculiar to Black Lady is that no hearts may be led until the third trick. This stops players passing on high hearts and then forcing them out straight away by leading low hearts.

Sevens

Players
Three to eight players. This is another good family game which doesn't take too long to play.

Cards
One full pack of fifty-two cards. Kings are high and aces are low.

Aim of the Game
The first player to get rid of all the cards in their hand is the winner.

How to Play
All the cards are dealt out one at a time. It doesn't matter if players have an extra card. The player to the dealer's left lays a 7 face up on the table if she or he has one, or if not, play passes along until a player does. The next player can either lay a 7 next directly above or below the first card, or play a 6 or an 8 of the same suit to either side of it. Again, if she or he has none of those options, play passes along.

So, if the first card to be played was the 7 of clubs, then the next player can play the 7 of hearts, spades or diamonds above or below the 7 of clubs, or the 6 or 8 of clubs to the left or right of the 7 of clubs respectively.

As the game progresses, four rows of cards will be built up by suit from left to right.

This is a tactical game. At the beginning, most players will have a choice of cards to lay but should try and encourage the building of sequences in the suits where they hold the highest and lowest cards – the king, ace, queen and 2 – so they are not left with isolated cards which cannot be played.

Players can also 'block' runs, by holding onto the relevant cards. For example, if you have the 7 of hearts, no other hearts can be played until you have laid it.

CARD GAMES FOR FOUR OR MORE PLAYERS

Three Card Brag
This is a famous precursor to Poker. It was popular with Elizabeth I and also Henry VIII, according to William Shakespeare.

Players

Between four and eight players is the ideal number though you can have more.

Cards

The full pack of fifty-two cards is used, with aces ranking high and 2s low.

Aim of the Game

To be in the lead when one player loses all their chips or money, or at a preagreed time for the game to end.

How to Play

Although extremely simple to play, Three Card Brag requires a little bit of preparation as well as some understanding of the ranking order of different card combinations.

Firstly, as in Pontoon, players should start with an equal bank of chips and agree a minimum and a maximum amount that can be 'raised' on each hand, as well as a total maximum bet for any player per hand.

The dealer deals each player three cards face down, places the remaining cards in a pile in the centre and then puts down the agreed minimum bet in front of him or her.

The player to the left now has three options: to either 'fold' or drop out by placing his or her cards face up on the pile; to stay in the round by putting an equal bet on the table; or to 'raise' by putting in the minimum bet and then adding a bet of his own.

The next player has the same options but, if the bet has been increased, the new amount must be matched or, of course, raised. All the players now follow, and the play continues on, going round the table until the deal ends with one of the following outcomes:

★ All the players reach the maximum bet for the hand. In this instance, all players show their cards to determine who has the best hand and collects the winnings.

★ All the players have bet an equal amount, but declined to increase their stake. Again, the cards are turned over to decide who the winner is.

★ Only one player remains in, the others having dropped out. He or she takes the total winnings for the hand.

★ With two players remaining, one can equal the bet laid by his opponent and challenge, 'I'll see you,' at which point the other

player must show his hand – win or lose – or concede defeat
without revealing his cards.

★ If no players decide to bet, then the dealer collects the minimum
stake from each of them, and the deal passes to the player on his
left.

The scoring for Three Card Brag is as follows, with the best hand
first. In all examples, aces count high and 2s count low, although for
running flushes and runs, ace, 2, 3 is the highest-scoring
combination, followed by ace, king, queen, with the lowest sequence
being 4, 3, 2.

★ Three of a kind: three 4s, jacks or aces, for example.
★ Running flush: three cards from the same suit in sequence, for
instance, 4, 5, 6 of hearts.
★ A run: three cards in sequence from different suits, say the jack
of hearts, queen of clubs and king of spades.
★ A flush: three cards of the same suit, for instance 4, 9 and jack
of clubs.
★ A pair: two cards of the same rank and another card, say two 6s
and a 3.
★ High card: the highest card in the hand of three where none
of the above combinations exist.

If two players have equal pairs, the highest third card determines
the winner.

Whist

*The rubber was conducted with all that gravity of deportment and
sedateness of demeanour which befit the pursuit entitled 'Whist' – a
solemn observance, to which, as it appears to us, the title of 'game' has
been very irreverently and ignominiously applied.*

Charles Dickens, *The Pickwick Papers* (1868)

Whist is another game with a long and proud tradition. It was a
favourite game in English high society in the eighteenth century,
when it was known as Whisk, for some strange reason. It was derived
from an even older game called Triumph, which gave us the word
'trump' – for the highest-ranking suit in cards.

As we can see from Charles Dickens's description, the game was
taken quite seriously in his day, and was tremendously popular in all

classes. Whist 'drives', which were held in villages across England to raise charitable donations, were the pub quizzes of their day. Whist was eventually superseded by Bridge in London high society, but remains one of our favourite card games with the advantage of being easy to learn.

Players

Four players – partners playing opposite each other. One player on each side should collect the tricks won by their partnership.

Cards

A full pack of fifty-two cards, with aces high and 2s low.

Aim of the Game

For your partnership to win more tricks than your opponents'. There are many ways of scoring Whist, but we've suggested an easy version to start with. Agree a target of game points to be reached by the winning side – twenty points is a good tally for a first attempt.

How to Play

The dealer deals the pack clockwise, one card at a time, face down, until the last card is reached which should be dealt face up. This is the dealer's last card and also dictates which suit is trumps for the game.

The player to the dealer's left now leads with the card of his or her choice. The three other players must follow suit if they can. If they can't then they may play any other card from their hand, including a trump card. When each person has played a card the first 'trick' is complete. It is won by the highest trump card or, if no trump has been played, then the highest card in the suit that was led wins the trick. The player who wins the trick leads the next one with the card of his or her choice.

When all the cards have been played, each partnership adds up the number of tricks it has won, discarding the first six. So if one partnership has won eight tricks, it gets two points towards its game points total. If a partnership wins fewer than six tricks in a hand, it simply gets no points rather than a negative score. The deal now passes to the player on the first dealer's left.

Although it is quite a simple game, players quickly learn that remembering which cards, and particularly trumps, have been played, and by whom, is important. There are other established strategies, like playing a trump if in possession of five or more, to flush the other trumps out. This gives the player a better chance of clearing up the later tricks, as she or he is less likely to be trumped.

SHUFFLING

In many games, patience games for instance, shuffling the pack is important to prevent cards appearing in the same sequence, hand after hand.

There are many methods of doing this, and we've included a couple of the easier ones, which can be picked up and used by anyone, regardless of experience. As with playing cards, or practically any skill, practice improves technique, and it's fun to learn these shuffles. It won't be long before you look like a real card sharp. They're described for right-handed people. If you're left-handed, simply reverse the instructions as necessary.

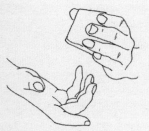

The Overhand Shuffle

This is an easy shuffle for beginners to pick up. You need to hold the pack of cards in your left hand, with the thumb resting against the top of the pack, and your middle, ring and small finger resting lightly against the bottom, or picture side.

Lift roughly the bottom half of the pack with your right hand, with your right thumb on the edge of the pack nearest you, and the right index, ring and little finger on the other end.

Bring the cards in your right hand up and then down in front of those held in your left. Release some of the cards and use your left thumb to press them to the cards already in your left hand. At the same time, lift the bottom half of the cards in your right hand, by retaining pressure on them with your right thumb and other fingers, and bring this diminished pile to the front, or top, of the pack in your left hand. Repeat the process of dropping some cards and retaining some in your right hand, until all the cards you originally lifted from the bottom of the pack, have been 'shuffled' into the top. Do this several times. The pack will be well shuffled.

The Table Riffle Shuffle

This is another good one for beginners and looks good too, if you can do it quickly. It's used a lot in casinos so if you can master this, you're on your way to being a pro!

Divide the pack roughly into two piles, face down. Hold half in each hand, with the middle, ring and little fingers pressed against the outside short edge of the pack, and the thumbs placed against, and slightly underneath, the inside short edge – the one nearest you. Your index fingers should be pressed down roughly in the middle of the two halves of the pack.

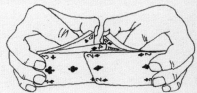

Use your thumbs to lift the inside short edge of each half of the pack, moving them close together as you do this.

Then 'riffle' the two halves together – release cards from the bottom upwards in an overlapping cascade. The corners of the cards from each half should mix together as you do this.

Now release your hold on the cards and push the two interwoven halves together, squaring them off as you do so. The pack should now be cut; with the bottom half replaced on the top half. There you go – a nicely shuffled pack.

CARD GAME AND BETTING TERMS

Cards, like any game that's played very widely, has a vocabulary all of its own. We thought it would be helpful to add a short section defining the different words used in descriptions of card play – both in this book and elsewhere.

* Ante: This is a compulsory amount of money paid by each player before the deal. It forms the basis of a kitty or pot.
* Bluff: If you bluff when you're betting at cards, you pretend to have a better hand than you actually hold.

* Fold: When you fold in cards it means you don't want to carry on betting. Usually this means that you lose whatever money you have contributed to the pot to that point.

* Raise: In betting, to raise is to match the highest current bid and add some extra. Players must either pay more money to see your cards or raise you again to keep the betting round going.

* Bid: A bid is a statement of how many tricks you think you can win in the hand just dealt.

* Card sharp/shark: In British English, it is still more normal to say 'card sharp'; whereas in American English 'shark' is more common. Both 'sharp' and 'shark' on their own date back centuries when applied to people who con you. The oldest reference we have is in Ben Jonson's *Every Man Out of His Humour* (1599) where Sordido is referred to as a 'thread-bare shark'. 'Sharp' is a little younger but by the eighteenth century meant someone who lived by his wits and took advantage of people. Curiously, the earliest sightings of both 'card sharp' and 'card shark' are American – from the late nineteenth century. Language experts approve of both terms, so there is no need to feel that you have to favour one over the other.

* Carte blanche: This technically means a hand that contains no picture cards.

* Dead hand: An extra hand which has no bearing on the game.

* Discard: To lay a card down that you no longer need or are compelled to by the rules of the game.

* Flush: In Poker and Brag, a hand of cards all in the same suit. A royal flush is ace, king, queen, jack and 10 of the same suit (the highest possible hand in Poker).

* Foundation: A card (usually in Patience) which acts as a base for building sequences on. It is usually held or placed separate from the pack.

* Meld: A group or a combination of cards that has value in the scoring system of a game.

* Misère: In Whist and other bidding games, a bid that you will take no tricks.

* Napoleon: The opposite of Misère, an undertaking that you are going to take all tricks in a hand.

* Natural: A set of cards containing no wild cards.

* Revoke: If you revoke in cards, you either fail to follow suit when you can or play a card which breaks the rules of the game.

* Round-the-corner: This means a sequence of cards (a run) that goes beyond the ace; so, queen, king, ace, 2 etc.
* Stock: The pile of cards which remains after the deal but will be called on later in the game.
* Tableau: Particularly used in Patience, it is the place where you lay your cards out on the table.
* Three of a kind: Three cards with the same number of pips on (or the same royal picture).
* Trick: The winning pile from one hand of cards in which each player plays one card.
* Trump: A suit that outranks the other three suits (usually just for one turn).
* Void: If you have no cards of one suit in a hand you are said to be void of that suit.
* Wellington: A bid that outdoes Napoleon.
* Widow: An extra hand.
* Wild card: A playing card that can represent any card designated by the holder.

The 9 of Diamonds

The Curse of Scotland is the 9 of diamonds. No one actually knows why it is so called. A number of theories have been advanced – some slightly more bonkers than others but here are the main ones:

* It is said that when Sir John Dalrymple, the Earl of Stair, ordered the Glencoe Massacre he did so using the 9 of diamonds as a code for authorisation. The theory is based on the fact that the card bears a strong similarity to his coat of arms.
* Before the Battle of Culloden, the Duke of Cumberland apparently gave the order for 'no quarter' (i.e. no mercy) to be given to the enemy written on this playing card.
* One theory that doesn't involve notorious bloody deeds from history suggests that it is a corruption from 'the Corse [i.e. Cross] of Scotland'. The Saltire and the 9 of diamonds do have a passing resemblance.
* One last unlikely theory is that it is named after a tax imposed on the Scots when a certain George Campbell stole nine diamonds from the crown of Mary Queen of Scots in the 1560s. The tax was levied to pay for the replacement jewels.

The consensus seems to be that the first explanation is the likeliest.

Dice Games

Dice evolved out of knuckle bones which were made literally of the knuckle bones of animals. Knuckle bones were used both for gambling and for divination. Legend has it that there were originally four heavy bells in the old St Paul's before Henry VIII gambled them on a throw of the dice ... and lost. Playing at dice seems to have been a constant throughout British history and, while its popularity may have fallen off over the past few years, there are many good games to play which are still worth remembering – and fun too.

ONE-DICE GAMES

Pig Dice

A very basic game that has many variations and names – a dicey (!) game in which players must gamble on whether to bank their points, or continue to throw and risk losing everything.

Players take it in turns to throw a dice and accumulate the points they rolled (the face value of each throw), continuing to throw until they decide to bank the points or throw a 1. If they throw a 1 then all the points they have accumulated are lost and the play passes to the next player.

If they decide to bank the points, their total is noted and play passes to the next player. The first to reach an agreed target number of points is the winner. A player who throws a 1 on his or her first roll must pass the dice to the next player – no cheating.

Dice Pontoon

This is a game for any number of players and works very much like the card game Pontoon. One player rolls the dice and continues to do so, keeping tally of the points rolled as he or she goes until close to thirty-six. Close to thirty or so he or she must decide whether to continue rolling or to 'stick' on the number reached. The closest to thirty-six (without exceeding that number) wins the pot if you are betting. If two or more players get thirty-six in one round then the pot remains for the next round.

Beetle Drive

Beetle Drive is a very easy dice and drawing game and very good for younger children. The aim of the game is to be the first to complete a drawing of a beetle based on the roll of a dice.

First show the children how to draw a simple beetle. The easiest has six different elements (antennae, head, eyes, body, legs and some markings on the back – see illustration). Each element corresponds to a number on the dice: so if a child throws a 1 then he or she gets to draw the appropriate part of the beetle's body.

1 – Body
2 – Head
3 – A Leg
4 – An Eye
5 – An Antenna
6 – Back markings

Give each child a dice and some coloured pencils. They take it in turns to roll the dice once and draw the element of the beetle that corresponds to the number they roll. But of course there is a logical sequence to this – for example it is not possible to draw the legs without having first drawn the body or the antennae without the head. They can only draw one item at a time; so if your beetle has two antennae and six legs then they must roll the number that corresponds to the antennae twice and the number that corresponds to the leg six times. The children take it in turns to roll and draw until one has completed the beetle and is the winner.

FIVE-DICE GAMES

Liar Dice
This is one of the classic dice games – apparently a favourite of pirates – and a game of gambling and bluff. Each player needs a set of five ordinary dice and a cup or something to roll the dice from. The aim of the game is to be the last player to have dice available to roll.

All players roll their dice and keep the outcome concealed from the others by either hiding the dice behind their hand or immediately covering the dice with the cup they used to throw them – in both cases the player has to take a sneaky look at their dice. One player commences with a bid which is a guess as to how many of a certain number have been rolled by all players. So 'seven

6s' or 'three 4s'. The next player has two options: to increase the bid according to the bidding rules or to call (challenge) the previous player's bid. If he or she increases the bid it is then the following player's turn to decide whether he wants to increase or challenge the preceding bid. The game continues with bids increasing until a challenge is made. When a bid is challenged all players' dice are revealed and the bid evaluated. If the number of faces that match the player's bid are fewer than the bid then the bidder loses; if they are equal or more then the challenger loses and once of his dice is removed for the next turn. So, if a player's bid of five 4s is challenged, the bidder loses if there are fewer than five 4s in the assembled dice from all the players; if there are five or more the challenger loses. In each case the losing player removes one dice from his set for the next and subsequent rounds.

There are many different bidding rules but the simplest is that any increased bid must be either in the number of a certain face – so three 4s must increase to a minimum of four 4s – or any number of a higher face so three 4s can become one 5 or three 5s but it cannot be four 3s. The player who doesn't lose all his dice is the winner.

A lot of games require a 1 to be wild – that is, it counts as the value of the current bid. So if someone bids five 4s, then 1s count as 4s when the dice are counted up.

A version of this is often played as a drinking game whereby every time a player loses, instead of having a dice removed, he takes a drink.

Drop Dead

This is a game where the target is to get a certain number of points as quickly as possible. It's good to play with young children to help with mental addition.

Using a set of five, the first player to go rolls all the dice, removing any 2s or 5s that appear, and adding up the value on the faces of the remaining dice. The same player then rolls again (without the dice which had landed on a 2 or 5 in the previous throw), removing any further 2s or 5s and adding the value of the remaining dice to the total from the previous round. This player carries on until he or she has no dice left. The five dice are then passed to the next player who plays the same way. The first to reach an agreed target – one hundred points, say – is the winner. If a player rolls only 2s and 5s then he or she has 'dropped dead' and is out.

Ship, Captain and Crew

This game is also known as Ship of Fools.

You can play this very popular gambling game with two or more players – though the more, in this case, is definitely the merrier. One player starts by rolling all five dice. The aim is to get a 6 (which represents the ship), a 5 (the captain) and a 4 (the crew) in that order. So, for example, if a player gets a 5 and a 4 in the first roll then they cannot use them because they need a 6 first of all. If they get a 6 on the next roll it is put to one side and the remaining four dice rolled. The player gets up to five rolls to make the ship, captain and crew. Once they have those three numbers, either on the turn when they are rolled or on subsequent ones if there are any left, the sum of the two remaining dice represents the value of the cargo.

For example:

★ Roll 1: 5, 4, 2, 1, 1. Player can't keep 5 or 4.
★ Roll 2: 6, 4, 4, 2, 1. Player can keep 6 but not 4.
★ Roll 3: 5, 4, 2, 1. Player can keep 5 and 4. Cargo value = three.
  Has to decide whether to stick on three or try to roll a bigger score with the next two rolls of the two remaining dice.
★ Roll 4: 4, 1. Cargo value = five.
★ Roll 5: 3, 1. Cargo value = four.

The player's cargo is worth four. Play passes to the next player who now has five rolls to beat this score, unless the first player decides to stop after three rolls, because she or he has rolled a 6, 5, 4 and a good cargo score. In this case, all subsequent players also only have three rolls to beat their score. If the first player doesn't manage to complete the set of ship, captain and crew then his or her cargo value is zero.

In order to bet, it is usual for all players to put an ante into the pot before the first player rolls. In the event of a tied cargo value at the end of the round, the pot can either be split the appropriate number of ways, or the players with the same value cargo can have a 'roll off' to decide the winner, or the pot can be held over to the next round. This last option makes for the most exciting game and keeps everyone involved.

Variation: One nice variant of this game is that if anyone rolls 6, 5, 4, 6, 6 on their first roll (called a 'midnight') then that player automatically takes the whole pot.

Yacht (also known as General and Yahtzee™)

This is a great game for families. The idea is to try to complete a number of different combinations of dice while scoring the most points. Before the first player rolls the dice, all players should draw up a table of combinations of dice and how many points they are worth.

Suggested scoring card layout:

Upper Section	Player 1	Player 2	Player 3	Player 4	Player 5	Scoring instruction
Total all 1s						Each count one, max score = five
Total all 2s						Each count two, max score = ten
Total all 3s						Each count three, max score = fifteen
Total all 4s						Each count four, max score = twenty
Total all 5s						Each count five, max score = twenty-five
Total all 6s						Each count six, max score = thirty
Three-of-a-kind						Value of three matching dice (i.e. Three of a kind of 2 = six points)
Four-of-a-kind						Value of four matching dice (i.e. four of a kind of 5 = twenty points)
Full house						Total value of dice
Low straight						1, 2, 3, 4, 5 (thirty points)
High straight						2, 3, 4, 5, 6 (forty points)
Five-of-a-kind						Fifty points regardless of value of five-of-a-kind number
Chance						No pattern but each player must complete a round in which the score is the total value of the dice
Grand total						

The first player rolls the five dice, and, depending on how the dice land, decides which combination he or she is going to go for. He has two more turns to complete the combination (but can stop after one or two turns if satisfied with what he has got), only rolling the discards (the dice that don't fit into the combination he is going for) on subsequent turns. The player can change this chosen combination at any stage. If he rolls 1, 1, 2, 3, 5, for example, he might decide to go for 1s but with the next roll he might get 6, 6, 6 and decide to go for either full house, or three, four or five of a kind. If he does decide to change he can bring back the dice already set aside to complete the combination he wanted to try to complete on the last roll.

There are twelve rounds in each game – one for each of the scoring combinations. The player with the biggest total at the end of the twelve rounds wins.

SIX-DICE GAMES

Farkle

Farkle is great fun – even its name makes you smile – and extremely popular. There is a Facebook page dedicated to it which has 2.8 million users and 350,000 'fans'.

It's usually played with six dice and the aim is to be the first to score an agreed number of points. You get points by rolling combinations of dice. A turn can consist of any number of throws and you score points by throwing combinations of dice, banking (i.e. putting to one side and not using in the next throw) good ones as you go. See the examples below.

The trick with this game is knowing when to stop: as you roll and make combinations you have to judge the point at which it is safer to keep the points you have accumulated in your turn than to keep on rolling. If you roll and cannot make a new combination you get a 'farkle', lose all the points in that turn and pass the dice to the next player. If, however, you manage to combine all six dice then you are said to have 'hot dice' and can have another turn.

Faces 1 and 5 score points on their own while the other combinations and their points score are detailed below.

Farkle scoring table

Each 1	=	100 points
Each 5	=	50 points
Three 1s	=	1,000 points
Three 2s	=	200 points
Three 3s	=	300 points
Three 4s	=	400 points
Three 5s	=	500 points
Three 6s	=	600 points
Straight (1, 2, 3, 4, 5, 6)	=	1,000 points
Six of a kind	=	instant victory!

Each roll is scored separately. If you were to roll two 5s for 100 points, then if you rolled a 5 on the next roll, you would not get 500 points for three fives, you would get another 50 points for a total of 150 points. Some variations require a player to score 1,000 points in one turn before they can get on the scoreboard proper.

Examples

You throw 1, 2, 3, 3, 3, 5. You can score in any of the following ways:

★ You could just keep 1 for 100 points.
★ Or 1 and 5 for 150 points.
★ 3, 3, 3 for 300 points.
★ 1, 3, 3, 3 for 400 points.
★ 1, 3, 3, 3, 5 could be kept for 450 points.

If you took any of the first four options, you would probably throw the remaining dice to see if you could score further; but in the case of scoring the fifth option, you could either bank the points and pass the dice, or throw the remaining dice, with a one-in-three chance of scoring (getting a 1 or 5). If you were to score, you could bank your final score and pass the dice, or throw all six dice again, and further increase your score.

You roll 1, 2, 2, 5, 6, 6. You keep the 1 and the 5 for 150 points. You then opt to roll the remaining four dice. On that roll you get 1, 2, 3, 3. You could select the 1 and decide to pass and bank your points. You could continue to play with the remaining three dice but if you throw again at this point you are hoping to get either a 1 or a 5 or three of the same number.

Normal target scores are anything up from 12,000 points – depending on how long you want to play.

CHRISTMAS
and NEW YEAR
Games and Pastimes

The Christmas holidays are the classic time of year for families to gather together and play games. Our family was no exception. Most years, Daisy would get the coach to Victoria to be collected by Dad and brought home for the duration. I suspect we enjoyed her visits more than our parents, by and large, and one of the highlights was that nearly every evening became games evening. Sure, we had squabbles over rules, cheating and who ate the last crisp, but there's no shortage of good memories – of the almost impossible excitement of Christmas itself, which the games somehow restoked as darkness fell.

Here we've included some classics, like Charades, but also some more unusual diversions we uncovered, like the Victorian Body Challenges – a good way to stretch out after the festive slump. There are also a couple of seasonal recipes to keep you sparkly into the New Year.

Christmas Decorations

*It was Queen Charlotte, the consort of mad King George III, who introduced
decorative 'Christmas trees' to England from her native Germany in the
eighteenth century. Ironically it is thought that the practice probably originates
from pagan traditions of adorning hibernating trees to encourage strong, new
growth.*

*Prince Albert made Christmas decorations more popular and the Victorians,
or at least the fairly wealthy ones, took up the challenge of making yuletide
ornaments with some relish.*

Making an Orange Pomander

Pomanders date back to the Middle Ages when perfume balls,
or *'pommes d'ambres'* (literally 'apples of amber'), would be worn
or carried for their supposed power to guard against airborne
infections. They probably weren't much use, but they certainly
made the air smell nicer.

This orange pomander is simple to make and will give out a
pleasant, spicy odour over the festive season and way beyond. Not
recommended as a preventative against flu or any other illness.

Orris root can be bought from health food shops, and craft shops.

You will need

1 medium-sized orange
Around 25g (1oz) cloves
1 teaspoon orris root powder
1 teaspoon ground cinnamon
Some non-adhesive tape and some decorative ribbon of roughly
    the same width
Some pins to hold the tape in place
A wooden skewer, or cocktail stick
A paper bag

Run the tape around the orange in two lengths, so it divides the
surface into quarters. Pin the tape in place.

Pierce the orange skin all over with the wooden skewer and press
the cloves into the holes (using the skewer saves your fingertips from
getting bruised). You can either completely cover the surface or
create a nice pattern with the cloves.

Mix the orris root and ground cinnamon together and roll the
orange in them. Put the orange and the spices into a paper bag, and

keep it somewhere warm and dry for several weeks – an airing cupboard is an obvious place. As an added bonus, your clothes should begin to smell lovely.

When the orange has dried out, take out the pins and remove the tape. Carefully wrap the decorative ribbon around the orange, where the tape was, and secure with a bow. The pomander can now be attached to a Christmas tree, or elsewhere, by tying some thread through the bow.

Games for Christmas and New Year

ACTING GAMES

Charades

This is a classic parlour game for any family occasion and for all ages. Sure to guarantee a very raucous hour or two.

Divide the players into two teams. On a small slip of paper, each player writes the title of a film, play, book, song, television or radio programme, character (either a fictional character, a historical figure or a living personality) or quote – the choice is yours, but if playing with younger children it is best to avoid anything that they won't be familiar with.

Each team puts their subjects into a separate hat and hands it to the opposing team.

The first player to act out a charade chooses a slip from the opposing team's hat, and must act out the title or phrase (in mime) to his or her own team, in the following order:

★ Describe the type of subject
★ Show how many words are in the title
★ Indicate which word you are acting and then get going

A timer may be set to heighten the pace and excitement of the game.

If the actor succeeds and her team guesses correctly within the given time, they score a point. It is then the turn of a player from the opposing team to pick a subject from the hat.

The game continues until all players have had a turn, or until all the subjects have been acted.

The team with the most points wins.

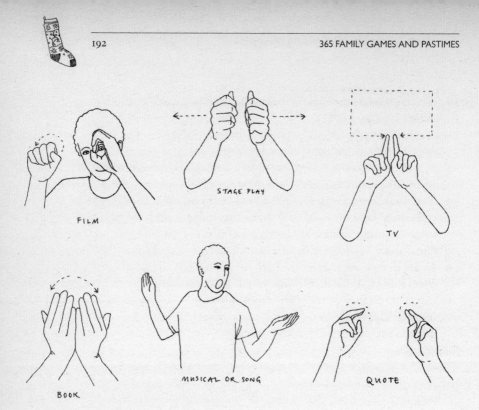

The Mimes

Describing the Category of your Charade

★ Film: A winding movement with the hand to indicate an old-fashioned camera.
★ Stage play: Mime as if you're pulling apart curtains on a stage.
★ Television show: Mime a large square shape round your face to represent a TV screen.
★ Book: Hands held together in front of you, then opened like a book.
★ Musical or song: Stretch your arms wide and vigorously mime operatic singing – you can also get down on one knee, for added theatricality.
★ Quote: Make quotation marks in the air with your fingers.
★ Character: Stand with your hands on your hips, then raise one finger for a male, two for a female character.

Communicating with Your Team

★ Number of words: Hold up the appropriate number of fingers. To indicate which word you are acting next, again hold up the relevant number of fingers. So if third word, hold up three fingers, and so on.

★ If you are going to act the whole subject in one go, draw a huge circle in the air.
★ Number of syllables in a word: Press corresponding number of fingers of the right hand on the left arm.
★ To indicate which syllable of a word, follow the mime above with a new number of fingers shown, three fingers for third syllable, etc.
★ Sounds like: Hold your ear with thumb and forefinger of one hand.
★ Little word or long word: Use index finger and thumb to indicate something tiny. Hold arms wide to indicate a big word.
★ Plural word: Link the little fingers together.
★ To encourage the guessers to keep on guessing in the same vein: Turn your right hand over and over, nodding vigorously.
★ Correctly guessed word or the whole charade: Index finger of right hand on tip of nose and point to the person who has shouted out correctly with the left hand.

LITTLE WORD

SOUNDS LIKE

3 SYLLABLES

Some Basic Rules
★ No sound should be uttered by the actor
★ The actor should not point to any object or person in the room to help describe a word in the subject
★ The guessers can ask questions of the actor but the actor can only nod or shake his head as a response.

Variation: For a more grown-up gathering, or to make things a little trickier, you could decide that the subjects may only be from a specific or more obscure subject area – historical figures, Irish novels, names of paintings – anything goes as long as you are playing with a group of like-minded people.

Proverb Charades

A variant of standard Charades where the subject to be acted is always a proverb.

Shadowgraph

This is a ghostly form of Charades acted out behind a screen so that only a shadow can be seen – good for long winter nights or Halloween.

Form a screen by hanging a large white sheet across part of the room, place a table light behind the sheet, and darken the rest of the room.

Each player takes it in turns to stand behind the sheet to mime an action or charade to the others. As only a shadow can be seen by the audience, this makes it all the harder for them to guess correctly.

If there is a piano in the room, get someone to accompany the mime for added atmosphere.

French Charades

This game is a bit like a mime equivalent of Chinese Whispers and always ends up with completely bizarre interpretations, making it great fun. It requires much more of a team effort than ordinary Charades, and is best if played with older teenagers or adults.

Players form two teams. One team leaves the room, while the other team decides on a scenario to be acted out.

One player from the other team is called back in and is told what the scenario is.

A second player is then called in, and the first must act out the scenario to the second.

The second player then calls in a third player and acts out the scenario to him or her.

And so on until the last person has been performed to – who then has to guess what the scenario is.

If he or she cannot guess, the very first player is allowed to perform the mime again to see if his team can guess the original scenario correctly.

If not, the team who suggested the scenario wins a round.

Some suggestions of scenes to act out:

★ Attending the Oscars, waiting for the name to be called out, winning, walking up to the stage, accepting the prize, making your speech.

★ Taking your driving test with all the preparations and rehearsal as
   well as the test itself.
★ Pretend to be sitting in a dentist's waiting room, getting called for
   your appointment, walking to the chair and having a filling or
   some dental work done.

In the Chosen Manner

This game is suitable for four or more people to play at the same time.
One player, the questioner, leaves the room while the others discuss
and decide upon an adverb which can be illustrated by performing
an action, for instance, 'joyously', 'dramatically', or 'guiltily'.

The questioner then re-enters the room, and begins asking
the group questions, to discover the adverb. The first person can
be asked, for instance, 'Will you close the door, *in the chosen manner?*'
or, 'Will you shake hands with player three, *in the chosen manner?*'
The questioner can go around the group a preagreed number
of times before being defeated. So, if there are six players, you
might agree that the questioner can ask each player a maximum
of two questions, or ten in total to guess the adverb correctly before
the next person has a turn. If he or she guesses in time, then he
leaves the room to be set another adverb. This game can be played
as a continuous competition or, for instance, you can keep a tally
of how many answers it took each player to guess three adverbs
correctly – though this obviously depends on the acting skills of
the group.

Dumb Crambo

This has a notable heritage, dating back at least to the fourteenth
century, when it was known as the ABC of Aristotle. In its present
form, it was a much-loved game of such historical figures as
Karl Marx, James Boswell and Robert Burns, the poet, who wrote,
'Amaist as soon as I could spell, I to the crambo-jingle fell.'

It is another acting game. This time half the players, the actors,
must leave the room, and the remaining group, the audience,
decides upon a verb which the others must act out. When the actors
return, they are given another verb which rhymes with the chosen
word. For instance, if the chosen verb is 'pray', then they might be
told 'bay' or 'lay'. The actors then leave the room once more, and
decide on three possible verbs which could be the correct answer,
and a way to act them out by mime. They then perform for the

audience. If the guess is wrong, the audience must hiss and boo, but if they are right then they clap and applaud, and the groups change places.

Memory Lapse

The players gather in a room and one player is selected to go out and have a memory lapse. He or she comes back into the room having changed something about his appearance that is wrong – watch upside down or on the wrong hand, shoelaces not tied or shoes on the wrong feet. In other words, something that might happen when you are suddenly distracted. The other players can only look – they can't ask questions or move from their seats. The one who is first to guess correctly is the winner.

DRAWING GAMES

Picture Charades

This is a fast-paced and fiercely competitive drawing game which requires a little planning in advance. You'll need to gather together a drawing pad and pencil for each player, a stack of scrap paper, cut into squares, a dice and an egg-timer or watch.

Firstly, decide on six subject areas – Celebrities, Film, Book, Song, Food and Country, for instance. It doesn't matter if some categories are more difficult, this will just add to the fun. Give each subject a number – so Celebrity: 1, Film: 2, and so on. Now write entries for each subject on the squares of scrap paper, so Wayne Rooney, Prince Charles and Lily Allen might be the celebrity entries. Aim to write about ten entries for each category, so you don't run out too quickly (though obviously this depends on the number of players).

Each category is allocated a number from one to six (to equate to the numbers on a dice), and sorted into piles.

Players form two teams, and one player rolls the dice and takes a paper from the relevant category pile.

He or she must draw a picture to represent the name or object on the slip of paper, and his team has one minute to guess what is being drawn – if they do they get a point.

Continue in turns until all the cards in the centre have been drawn.

Variation: For very young players, make the objects to be drawn much more simple – a cat, an ice cream, a baby, and so on – and place them in a hat to be picked randomly by the child.

Artists' Relay Race

This is a good team game for all ages over five, and with larger groups so that three or four reasonably sized teams can be formed.

You'll need a pile of large sheets of paper, like A3, and some drawing materials – pencils or crayons or pens.

One player should be nominated as game leader. He or she then stays in another room and prepares a list of about fifteen objects to be drawn – easy or difficult items depending on the age and abilities of participants – and writes each out clearly on separate cards or small scraps of paper.

Each team receives a piece of A3 paper and something to draw with. They each nominate a player to start and these first players run to the game leader to be shown the first object to draw.

They dash back to their teams and start to draw the object. No words, letters or numbers are allowed. The teams try to guess what the object being drawn is and whisper the answer to the drawer – they mustn't shout out though, otherwise they might give the answer to the other team. As soon as one member of the team has guessed correctly, that team member runs back to the game leader to be shown the second object to be drawn. She or he then starts to draw and so on until one team has drawn and correctly guessed each of the objects, and is declared the winner.

At the end of the game it's fun to display the two sheets of hurried drawings.

VICTORIAN BODY CHALLENGES

These challenges are inspired by an old Victorian book of games, and require at least a degree of body flexibility, so probably best avoided if you have a bad back or iffy knee. Most children will love them though.

Knuckle Down

This is not very difficult unless the old knees are creaking a bit. Place the toes against a line chalked on the floor, kneel down and

get up again without using your hands, and without your feet having
moved from their original position.

Prostrate and Perpendicular

Cross your arms on your body, lie down on your back, and then get
up again, without using either your elbows or hands to assist you.

Catch Penny

Hold your right arm (or left arm if you are left-handed) up so that
your hand is touching your right shoulder and your forearm is
straight enough to balance three 1p or 2p coins about halfway along
it. Drop your elbow quickly and try to catch the money before it
falls to the ground. As you get better at this trick, you can increase
the number of coins to four or more. It's a good idea to practise on a
surface which won't encourage the coins to run off wildly, or drop
between gaps in floorboards.

Tantalus Trick

This is infuriating but good fun. Place your left leg and foot, and
your left cheek, up against a wall. Now lift your right leg slowly, and
try to bring it over to touch the left knee. Sounds easy? Try it.

The Triumph

We wouldn't even attempt this – probably a lot easier if you're
double-jointed. With your arms behind your back, bring the palms
together with the thumbs against your back and your fingers
pointing down.

Now attempt to turn your hands 'inside out' – raising them so that
your fingertips are pointing upwards and between your shoulders,
with the thumbs on the outside and your palms still together. Unless
you are extremely supple, and do a lot of yoga, this may take a lot of
practice – so don't rush into it, but take it gently and stop if anything
starts to hurt.

Jumping Over a Pencil

These Victorians must have been made of rubber. Hold a pencil
between your left and right forefingers, and try to jump over it –
forwards and backwards, without dropping it, or kicking it out of
your hands.

CANDIED FRUIT PEEL

In Tudor times, the wealthy British developed a very sweet tooth and a penchant for elaborate desserts. Cooks would make model animals, wine glasses and playing cards out of sugar and these confections were paraded at banquets as a sign of status and sophistication – sugar was a very expensive ingredient. The downside was an increase in tooth decay. Like many nobles, Elizabeth I's teeth are said to have become rotten and black as a result of her dessert addiction.

Fruit was also a luxury and, just as now, items like lemons and oranges had to be imported, though it took a little longer in those days.

Crystallised fruit peel was one of the dishes served at costly banquets and a very tasty one as well. We've included it here because it's a nice treat to make in the early spring, before there's much growth in the garden, and it gives a little taste of the sunshine that we know is long overdue. It doesn't require much in the way of ingredients or cooking proficiency, but it does take a little while to prepare, so maybe make this while doing something else in the kitchen.

You will need

Orange, grapefruit or lemon peel – the amount depends on
 the size of the fruit but three medium-sized lemons, or two
 medium oranges, or one grapefruit should be roughly equivalent
 to each other
250g white sugar – either granulated or caster is fine

Cut the top and bottom from the fruit, then cut the peel into large strips, making sure to keep as much pith as possible attached to the skin. Put in a saucepan with cold water to cover. Bring to the boil and then simmer for five minutes. Drain the peel and rinse it in cold water, then repeat the boiling, simmering and draining process two or more times, or until the peel is very soft. Grapefruit peel may take longer because of its thickness. Leave to cool.

When cool enough to handle, slice the peel into thinner and smaller strips.

Make a syrup in a small heavy-based saucepan by slowly heating and dissolving the sugar in 250ml of water.

Put the peel in the syrup and simmer on a very low heat, stirring occasionally, until the syrup is absorbed and the peel is gooey but still intact. This may take two hours or more – again it depends on the quality and thickness of the fruit.

Cover a wire rack with greaseproof paper and arrange the peel in a single layer to allow it to dry. Put in a warm, dry place and leave overnight, or longer if possible, before dipping in sugar. It is now ready for decorating cakes and puddings with. You can also dip and coat the sugared peel in melted chocolate, then allow to set. This makes a lovely gift.

FIRST FOOTING

As midnight strikes on 31st December the tradition of waiting for and welcoming the first person to call at your house – First Footing – begins.

This visitor is supposed to bring good fortune for the year ahead in the form of his person and with the gifts he carries. Tradition dictates that it should be a 'he'. We don't know why, but women First-Footers are thought to bring bad luck. More specifically the 'he' should be dark-haired – blond or fair-skinned men were a reminder of the Viking raids and they never brought good luck.

The gifts that the First-Footer brings are now symbolic but in times past they had a practical value too. Whisky, bread, salt, a silver coin and a lump of coal represented food, wealth and warmth. The coal was particularly welcome and was placed ceremoniously on the family fire with the words, 'May your hearth never grow cold.' (Coal was not only a symbol of warmth but has always been thought to be lucky – for this reason soldiers would often carry a piece of coal into battle with them.)

There are regional variations to First Footing but they all share the belief that what you are doing at New Year, or Hogmanay, determines your luck for the rest of the year.

First Footing is still prevalent throughout the British Isles: a recent survey showed that nearly a third of people in Britain still include the custom as part of their seasonal celebrations. Happy New Year!

MARMALADE

Although considered quintessentially British, beloved of expats
the world over, it is likely that 'Marmalade' came into the English
language via the Portuguese and then French words for a quince
preserve. It is dated in the *Oxford English Dictionary* as appearing
for the first time in 1480 and has, over the centuries, become a
firm fixture of British breakfast life. Although marmalade is usually
taken to be a preserve made from oranges, it can be made from a
wide range of ingredients, though usually citrus fruits provide the
main flavour.

Bizarrely, considering the fruit has never been grown there, orange
marmalade is claimed by some to be a Scottish invention. The story
goes that a James Keiller bought some Seville oranges from a ship
sheltering in Dundee from a severe storm, and gave them to his wife
who made chunky marmalade with the bitter Spanish fruit. It was
such a success that the couple opened the first commercial
marmalade business in 1797.

True story or not, every January tons of sour, inedible Seville
oranges are happily exported by grateful Spanish growers to
Britain, to brighten our darkest hours and give the kitchen a
warm, exotic glow.

*Tell Mrs Boswell that I shall taste her marmalade cautiously at first …
Beware, says the Italian proverb, of a reconciled enemy. But when I find
it does me no harm, I shall then receive it and be thankful for it, as a
pledge of firm, and, I hope, of unalterable kindness. She is, after all,
a dear, dear lady.*

Samuel Johnson to James Boswell, 1777

The world's Original Marmalade Festival is held in Cumbria each
year, attracting eight hundred entries in 2010, so it's clear we still
have an affinity for this delicious preserve. Although people now
experiment with cumquats, bananas and ginger to make their
favourite spread, we've stuck by the simple recipe our mother used
to make Seville Orange Marmalade – a highlight of any number
of cold, dark winter weekends.

You will need
1kg Seville oranges (about ten)
2kg sugar
2.5 litres water

A large casserole or preserving pan
Clean, sterilised jam jars
Wax discs, jam-jar covers and elastic bands for sealing

Simply put the whole oranges in a pan with the water and bring to the boil. Simmer the fruit slowly for about ninety minutes until the fruit can be easily pierced.

Turn the heat off, and take the fruit out of the pan, reserving the water, and leave to cool until the oranges can be handled with ease.

Now bring the water back to the boil, halve the oranges and remove all the pips – this can be quite a fiddly job and takes a little time. As you remove the pips, put them in the water.

Boil the water with the pips for ten minutes then remove them with a sieve or strain the water, throwing the pips away but keeping the cooking liquid in the pan. Meanwhile, cut the oranges into small chunks – the size is up to you as there will be those lovely bits you get to spread over your toast. We like quite thick pieces!

Add all your orange bits to the water, together with any leftover pulp, and bring to the boil before adding all the sugar. Cook gently until the sugar has dissolved, and then boil rapidly until the setting point is reached.

You can tell that the setting point has been reached in a number of ways. The easiest is to buy a cook's thermometer which will most likely have a mark at 105°C, 220°F, to indicate this point.

There are a couple of other reliable methods for judging whether the marmalade is ready. Once it has thickened slightly, spoon a small amount onto a cold plate and if, after a few seconds, it wrinkles when you prod it, the marmalade should set. The other test is to dip a wooden spoon into the marmalade, hold it horizontally over the pan for a few seconds and then tip the marmalade back in. If a flake forms on the edge of the spoon, the marmalade is, again, ready.

Turn the heat off and stir so that the orange chunks are evenly distributed. Spoon or pour the jam into warmed and sterilised jam jars, cover and seal. We wash our jars thoroughly in hot, soapy water, rinse and then dry them in a low-temperature oven, making sure that the jars aren't touching, as this may cause them to crack.

You can buy packs of jam-jar covers for 450g and 900g jars from hardware stores and kitchen shops. While the marmalade is still hot in the jars, place a wax disc on top of the preserve, with the wax side face down touching the marmalade. Then moisten one of the jam-jar covers and place over the mouth of the jar, moistened side up, and secure this with an elastic band.

Don't forget to label the jars with the date and the contents. Marmalade can last for years, if kept in a dry, dark location, and it's fun to remember the day you made a particular batch.

MAGIC

Once a staple of every father's repertoire and a guaranteed passion of every eight-year-old, performing 'magic' tricks has fallen out of favour a little recently. We had a Christmas box of tricks which, at a tender, less cynical age, seemed to offer something more than just entertainment – it promised to bridge the gap between a game of cards and the magical sleight of hands we goggled at on TV shows.

Most descriptions of magic tricks are prefaced with exhortations to practise to the point of obsession before you try any of them in public. Take it as read that, depending on how competent a 'magician' you want to appear, you at least need to practise to the point where you are comfortable with the trick. One other useful piece of advice, tailor your tricks to your audience: if you're confronted by a party of thirty exuberant eleven-year-olds, it's unlikely that you'll be able to a) keep their attention for very long or b) persuade them not to look at what you're trying to conceal up your sleeve. Be warned!

A Quick Magic Show for Children

If the entertainer you've booked for the children's party fails to materialise,
this little routine will earn you about half an hour's respite from the
demanding hordes. Some take a little preparation and be sure to only perform
those tricks you feel fluent in – there are few less forgiving audiences than
a birthday crowd of six-year-olds who are expecting a proper magician.

Think of a Number

This is a good one to get things going. Give one child (perhaps
the one whose party it is) a pen and a piece of paper. Ask him
or her to think of a number but not to tell you. Then ask her to
write out the following sums (let's suppose the number she thought
of is 57):

Her age (let's suppose 11)	11
Double her age	22
Add 5	27
Multiply by 100	2,700
Divide by 2	1,350
Subtract number of days in a year	985
Ask her to add the number she first thought of	1,042

Now to her total add 115. The result (1,157) shows you her age (11)
and the number (57). Amazement all round.

Advantageous Wager

Ask a member of your audience to show you their watch. Have a
good look – pretend to be a jeweller or a pawnbroker if you want
– and then give an estimate as to its value. Offer then a bet to the
watch-owner (for an amount a lot less than the watch is worth) that
they will not answer, 'My watch,' to three consecutive questions.
First show them the watch and ask, 'What do I have in my hand?'
to which the answer is, of course, 'My watch.' Next pick up another
object and ask them what it is. If they don't say, 'My watch,' then
they've lost. If they do then try to throw them off the trail by saying,
'Looks like you're going to win; what do I get if I lose?' Rather
nicely, if they reply correctly, 'My watch,' then you get to keep
it (only joking of course) but if they don't answer correctly then
you win as well! Prepare to be pelted with whatever your audience
has to hand.

Climbing Through a Postcard

You'll need a normal-sized
postcard, a pair of scissors and
a sharp knife for the initial cut.

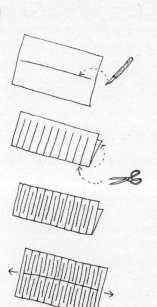

Announce to your audience
that you are going to cut a hole
in the postcard and climb
through it. Wait for the
disbelief. Then, on a suitable
cutting surface, cut a slit
lengthwise down the centre of
the card with the sharp knife,
taking care to stop before
reaching either end (see
diagram). The following cuts
can be made with scissors. Fold
the card over along the cut
(illustration 2) and cut a series of
lines through the card from the
line inwards but again never cut
beyond the edge. Turn the card around and cut between each of
the cuts you have already made. Stop before you get to the fold.

Now, with a lot of care, open up the fold and gently pull the ends
apart. The card will stretch out a long way and you can very slowly
wriggle through. (You can ask some of the audience members to
hold either end if you prefer.) Finish with a bow.

Upside-down Wine Glass

This is an old classic – simple to perform, but really worth practising
a few times before trying it out on your guests. The first few times
we tried we had some disappointed children and very wet feet.
Remember to practise over the sink as well!

You'll need a small wine glass – make sure the open end fits neatly
into the palm of your hand – and a small piece of ordinary writing
or printer paper cut in a square to amply cover the top of the glass.

Tell your audience that you can hold water in an upside-down
wine glass just using a piece of paper and one hand. Fill the glass
with water. Take the piece of paper, place it flat over the top of the
wine glass and hold it in place with the palm of your left hand
placed firmly and very flat on top. Take the wine glass in your right

hand by the stem. Keeping the palm of the left hand on the paper, invert the wine glass and keep your palm underneath the paper for about thirty seconds or so.

Withdraw your left hand and reveal that the paper remains in place and the water stays in the upside-down glass.

You can of course increase the drama by giving a witty commentary to your trick as you perform it, and ask the children to cast a spell before you remove your left hand.

The Impossible Knot-tying Trick

Ask one of the guests if he or she is good at tying knots. The challenge is, while holding (but never letting go of) both ends of either a tea towel or a handkerchief, to tie a knot in the middle of it. Without knowing how to perform this trick, it is impossible. When the chosen guest has had a go and given up, you can show the party how it is done.

Lay the tea towel down lengthways on a flat surface. Next fold your arms over it in the manner of the illustration below and grasp both ends. Then unfold your arms without releasing the ends and you'll find you have tied a knot!

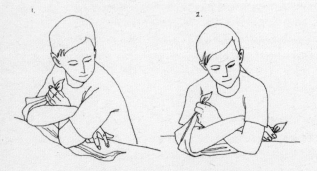

Drinking Wine Through a Hat

You'll need a wine glass filled with wine, and a hat.

Put a glass of your favourite wine on a table and cover it with a hat. Announce to the audience that you will empty the glass of wine without lifting the hat – make sure that there is at least one person who vociferously takes on the bet.

Tell the audience that under no circumstances may they touch the hat until you have finished, then get under the table and make a ridiculous spectacle of yourself as you pretend to drink the wine, with as many slurps and smacks of the lips as possible.

After an appropriate length of time, get out from under the table, wipe your lips and throw a challenging look at the person in the audience who took the bet.

She or he will either automatically pick up the hat to check whether the wine has been drunk or should do so with a tiny prompt from you, such as a cheeky nod towards the hat. As she lifts the hat to check, grab the wine and drink it.

You haven't touched the hat but have emptied the glass. *Voilà!*

Wet Coin – Dry Coin

This is a great trick to finish off the Magic Show. You'll need a dinner plate, a coin, some water, a slice from a wine cork (if you use a whole one it won't stay upright), some matches and an empty jam jar.

Put the plate on a table, put a coin on it (a 2p is fine) and cover the coin in water. Tell the audience that you can pick up the coin with your fingers without getting them wet. They won't believe you. Ask them to have a go if any claim they can.

Next produce your props. Force two matches into the cork slice so the match heads are pointing up. Float the cork on the water, away from the coin. Set light to the matches and when they are burning, invert the jam jar over them. After a couple of seconds, the matches will have gone out and, to everyone's amazement, the water will be sucked into the jam jar. With a flourish pick up the dry coin.

More Card Tricks

Finding the Card

This is a simple but puzzling trick for children. It sounds more complicated to perform than it is – follow the instructions on a couple of run-throughs and you will have mastered it in no time at all.

Ask a member of your audience to memorise a card as you deal three piles of seven cards face up in a row, so you have used twenty-one cards. Put the remaining cards in the pack to one side – you won't need them any more for this trick.

When you have finished dealing ask the audience member which of the three piles his or her card is in, without telling you which card it is, of course. Now turn over the three piles, so the cards are face down, and place the pile containing the memorised card between the other two piles.

Deal the twenty-one cards face up into three piles again and ask which pile the card is in now. Once more, turn the piles over and place the pile containing the memorised card between the other two piles. Repeat this process twice more. When your helper has told you which pile his card is in for the fourth time, turn the piles over as usual, place the pile containing the card between the other two and say, 'I will now reveal your card!'

Start turning the cards face up onto a table, appearing to think hard about each card. The eleventh one you turn up will be the memorised card. Perhaps you could muse over the card for a bit before saying, 'Yes, this is definitely your card.' It will be!

The world record for memorising cards is currently held by Canadian David Farrow who, in 2007, managed to memorise 3,068 cards (that's fifty-nine packs) with only one error. Incredible.

Obedient Cards

A great trick for an attentive children's party audience. Take your favourite suit of cards and arrange them face down in the following sequence – 3, 8, 7, ace, queen, 6, 4, 2, jack, king, 10, 9, 5 – with the 3 at the top and the 5 at the bottom of the pack.

Now tell your audience that by spelling the name of the cards out loud, in sequence from ace to king, they will bring the cards to the surface of the pack, one by one. Magic! Get your audience to begin calling out 'A-C-E' and each time they say a letter take one card from the top of the pack and move it to the bottom. After 'E', put up your hand to stop them chanting, and dramatically turn up the next card which will be the ace. Place that face up on a table for your audience to see and then get them to spell out 'T-W-O' as before. When the 2 comes up, place it face up next to the ace and continue. As long as you keep putting the cards back underneath, and turning up the card after the last letter has been called, the correct cards will appear.

Telling the Card

This trick relies on the fact that in any one shuffle it is highly unlikely that two cards become separated. It just doesn't happen that often which means that if you know the card that precedes the one that an audience member has selected it is nearly always possible to say that the next one is the one that has been singled out.

With that in mind, separate the pack into two roughly equal piles. Hold one pile in your left hand and the other in your right. Ask an audience member to take the left pile and select a card from it. The card is shown around and then placed back on top of the left pile. While the audience member and the rest of the audience are intent on the card selection, tilt the pack in your right hand slightly so that you can see the bottom card. Remember it. Have the audience member put the selected card back on top of the left-hand pack, put the right-hand pack on top of it and ask someone to shuffle the cards.

Once shuffled, take the complete pack back and start taking the cards off the top of the pack and placing them face up in front of your audience. As soon as you reach the card that was on the bottom of the right-hand pack you know that (unless you are really unlucky) the next card will be the selected card. You can build up to this moment as much as you like to make the 'reveal' as dramatic as possible.

Tricks with Matches

These tricks were developed over time in pubs in the days when smoking was compulsory – passive or otherwise. Times have changed to such a point now that you might be struggling to find a pub that sells matches, let alone one that allows you to perform tricks with them. The tricks below can, on the whole, be safely played in pubs or at home.

Vanishing Matches

All you'll need for this one are two boxes of matches and an elastic band.

You'll need to prepare just a little outside the room for this. Empty one of the matchboxes and leave the other half-full. Put an elastic band around the half-full one and attach it to your forearm under a long-sleeved shirt or jumper. Take the empty matchbox and shake it (with the arm that has the other matchbox secured to it, obviously!). Ask your rapt audience to guess how many matches there are in the box. After they have guessed, open it up and watch the surprise and bemusement on their faces.

There is a different version of this in which you place a full and an empty box on the table (with the half-full one still up your sleeve).

You can make the empty one appear to rattle by picking it up with the hand on which the secret matchbox is secured and then pick up the full one with your other hand. Being full it will not rattle; your (young) audience will wonder how you made an empty box rattle but a full one not.

The Cocktail Glass

This is a simple puzzle for your audience to scratch their heads over. You'll need four matches and one match head.

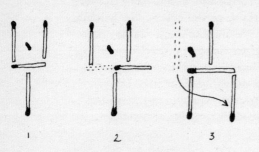

Arrange the matches as in fig 1. The olive in the glass is simply a match head.

The aim is, by moving only two matches, to remove the olive from the glass. They are not allowed to move the olive or change the shape of the glass. The solution is shown here in fig 3.

The Ring Snatch

You'll need two boxes of matches, a fine ring (or a penny) and (optional) a pair of tweezers.

This one is less of a puzzle and more of a trick that gets lots of lovely ooh's from everyone round the table. If someone is wearing a fine ring, use that rather than a penny. The idea is to show people that you can remove the object from under the diagonal match, as shown in the illustration.

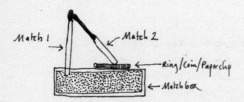

Set the trick up as shown. The upright match (match 1) needs to be pushed into the top of the matchbox so that it is held firmly in place. Put the object to be 'freed' a little distance away and then very carefully balance match 2 leaning against match 1 so that the match heads touch. This is where the tweezers come in handy – it helps to position the second match if you have shaky hands!

This trick also requires a good story – how could someone have stolen my ring when it was right there on my finger/my money when it was under my thumb? Use your imagination to build up the sense in your audience that this is impossible.

When you've left a little time for people to guess how to do it, produce the second box of matches. What happens next is great.

Light a match from the second box and either 1) light the two match heads on the first box or 2) light match 2 about halfway down its stem. If you go the first route, blow the flame out after a couple of seconds and you'll find the matches have fused together allowing you to remove the coin or ring. If you go the rather more satisfying second route, your audience will watch in amazement as the lower end of match 2 (the one securing the ring/coin) slowly bends upwards from the middle not unlike a dog cocking its leg. After it has bent sufficiently far up, you can easily remove the object underneath. If you perform this trick in the pub, you can get everyone to buy you a drink as a result!

Handkerchief Tricks

Handkerchiefs are out of fashion now. No longer do we carry our slightly crusty piece of cloth around for instant nose maintenance or for tying knots in to remind us of things; instead in our disposable society we have paper tissues. The problem with these is that you can do very little with them but with a handkerchief, well, the possibilities are legion. Here is one of the best-known and, once mastered, most satisfying tricks.

The Handkerchief Mouse

This was one of Lewis Carroll's favourite tricks. The folding procedure takes a bit of practice, but is very satisfying and can keep children amused and temporarily distracted if they have an obsession with owning a real pet. Well, it's worth a try.

Take your clean handkerchief and place it on a flat surface so it makes a diamond shape. Fold it so that the corner nearest you moves to touch the corner furthest from you – making a triangle whose bottom line is closest to you. Next take the two points of the bottom line of the triangle and fold them into the centre. They don't have to touch, merely to make a shape like an open envelope.

Now with both hands roll the handkerchief up as tightly as you can moving from the straight bottom of the envelope towards the open flap. It's quite important to get it as tight as you can. Stop about 7 or 8cm from the top of the flap. Flip the hankie over so the roll is underneath.

Fold the ends of the roll into the middle (like you did to make the envelope before) and then roll the folded ends over once towards the top corner. Take the top corner and fold it back towards you before tucking it into the fold at the top.

1.

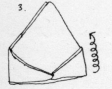

2.

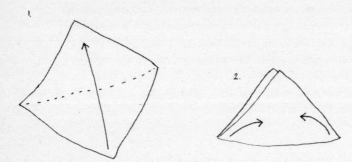

3.

4.

5.

6.

7.

8.

9.

10.

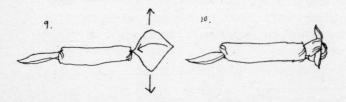

Dig your thumbs into the pocket closest to you and carefully roll the handkerchief inside out. Keep on doing this until you can't unroll any further. The two ends should have become quite visible. Holding on to the body gently draw out the ends so that you have something that looks a bit like a sausage with two thin tails. Tie a knot in one end to form the head (and you can pinch out the very ends to make them look like ears). You now have your mouse.

There are various ways of animating your new pet. The best and simplest is to cradle the mouse in the palm of your right hand. Have its head leaning against your thumb and its bottom supported by your middle finger. Gently stroke the mouse with your left hand and, as your left hand covers the middle finger of your right hand, quickly crook that finger and the mouse will shoot up in the air. If you are very devoted you can practise until you can get it to jump on to your shoulder every time.

Who needs a smelly kitten?

Victorian Mathematical Teasers

The Victorians loved their maths puzzles. Here's a selection of brainteasers which double up as magic tricks at a party.

Odd or Even?

Get a friend to divide a pile of coins so that she or he is holding an odd amount in one hand, and an even amount in the other. Tell her you can predict which hand has the odd number of coins, and which one has the even number. It doesn't matter how many coins she has in total.

Ask her to multiply the number of coins in her right hand by any odd figure, and the number in her left hand by any even one. Now ask her to add these two sums together and tell you whether they produce an odd or even total.

If the total is even, then the even number of coins is in her right hand, but if the total is odd, then the even number is in the left hand.

Here's an example:

Unbeknown to you, she has five coins in her right hand and six coins in her left.

She multiplies the coins in her right hand by an odd number (5 x 5 = 25) and the coins in her left hand by an even number (6 x 2 = 12).

By adding the two sums together she gets a total of 37, which means the even number of coins, you tell her, is in her left hand – correct!

Mind Reader
Impress with your ability to read a friend's mind!

Ask him or her to think of a number in his head, and to triple it (e.g. **9** x 3 = 27). Now ask him to divide the new figure in half and triple that number – if it's an odd number, then he should triple the nearest whole number upwards of the exact half figure (e.g. if it's 27, then he should take the number to be tripled as 27 ÷ 2 = 13.5, therefore the number he should use next is 14. **14** x 3 = 42).

Now ask him to calculate how many nines will fit in this new total (9 x **4** = 36).

To find the number he thought of, simply double the figure (4) and add one (4 x 2 = 8 + 1= **9**).

Present him with your answer, conferring as much mystery on the process as you can!

Variation: For added effect, you can offer to once more read his thoughts. Tell him to think of another number, double it, add 4 to this figure, and then multiply the new figure by 5. Now pause for effect, and to give him a breather, and then tell him to add 12 and then multiply this total by 10. Finally he should deduct 320 from the new figure and tell you the remaining total.

Ratchet up the drama – press fingers to your closed eyelids, furrow your brow and simply take the last two figures away from this total to give you the figure he thought of!

Here's a demonstration with the method highlighted:

The figure is 15.

15 **x 2** = 30

30 **+ 4** = 34

34 **x 5** = 170

170 **+ 12** = 182

182 **x 10** = 1,820

1,820 **− 320** = 1,500

1,500 **minus last 2 figures** = 15.

Magic!

Predicting Two Numbers

Ask someone to think of two numbers between 1 and 9 – it can be the same number twice – two 3s for instance. Tell him or her to write the two numbers down on a piece of paper which is hidden from your view.

Now ask her to double the first number she thought of and add 1 to the sum. Next, she should multiply the new total by 5 and then add the second number she thought of. Ask her what the new total is.

By subtracting 5 from this you will have her two numbers in the order she thought of them. Present your answer with a flourish. Maybe press on the piece of paper, as if reading the contents through your fingertips!

Here's an example:

The two numbers thought of are 7 and 8.

$7 \times 2 = 14$
$14 + 1 = 15$
$15 \times 5 = 75$
$75 + 8 = 83$
$83 - 5 = 78$ (7 and 8).

WORD GAMES

Word games are instant, portable entertainment. In this selection of our favourites the only equipment you'll need is some paper, pens and a bit of linguistic bravura. Some of these games have been around for centuries and all are very simple. They rely less on ingenuity than the ability to enter into the spirit of game-playing and being able to laugh at yourself, as well as your nearest and dearest. From that point of view, they have been selected so that any age group can play them, anywhere, at any time – after breakfast, before tea or with a nice glass of wine in front of a roaring fire.

Written Word Games

Hangman

A classic game for all ages – great to play with younger children as they start to learn to write and spell, as it's not only a lot of fun but also a sneaky way of practising spelling.

For older children and adults, the game can be made more complex by nominating a category of word, name or phrase to be guessed – book titles, songs, famous actors, characters from films, and so on.

You can make the frame for your 'gallows' and the victim as rudimentary or as elaborate as you like depending on how many guesses you want to allow per word or phrase.

One player decides on a word or phrase and marks out the letters as shown, indicating a new word in a phrase with an oblique (/) as below.

```
----/---/----
```

The other player suggests a letter which may or may not be in the word. If the letter is in the word, then it is filled in. If it is not, a part of the gallows is drawn for each wrongly guessed letter. When the gallows is complete, and the word is still not correctly guessed, a body part of the hanged man is drawn for each letter not in the word.

The guesser keeps suggesting letters until either the word is guessed correctly, or until the gallows and victim is fully drawn, at which point the Hangman has won and the guesser has lost the game.

Composite Stories

An excellent game for five or so creative players. The players decide on a title for a story and each player writes an opening paragraph. The stories are passed on to the next player who adds a paragraph (say in five minutes) and so on until it gets back to the first player who has to finish the story off. To spice this up a bit, you can get each player, before the writing starts, to add the name of a famous person (or one familiar to all the players) to the top of the page. When the players get to start each story they find that there are a number of people who have to be introduced to the story.

Categories

A game that requires the ability to think quickly under pressure.

Before the game starts, each player writes (on separate scraps of paper) up to five categories or themes – animals, plants, countries, games etc. These are placed in a bowl. Each player has a sheet of paper and pen. One player calls out a letter of the alphabet and another picks a category at random from the bowl.

The players then have an agreed amount of time (use an egg timer if you have one, and turn it to start the game) to write down as many words as they can relating to that category starting with the chosen letter.

You can keep scores by simply adding up the number of correct answers each player gets. The winner is the first to reach fifty points, or more or less, depending on how long you want the game to last.

Categories II

A common variation of this is to think up collectively, say, fifteen categories – for example, flowers, historical characters, rivers, animals, something small enough to fit inside a matchbox, a world record holder etc. The narrower the category, the better. On a piece of landscape paper, players write the categories down the side, and as many columns as there are rounds to be played across the sheet.

One player then opens a book at random and calls out the first letter on the page. All players then have fifteen minutes or so to think of a word beginning with that letter for each of the categories. Wait for the arguments to start as you pass your piece of paper to the left to mark the round.

Scoring: three points for a word that no one else has; two points if it is shared with one other player; one point if three players have the same word. No points scored if more than three players have written the same word.

Fictionary

This one is great fun if you're feeling very creative. The rules are very similar to Call My Bluff, with each player in turn selecting an obscure word from the dictionary. This game is the basis for Balderdash and is also known more simply as the Dictionary Game or Dictionary. To play it you'll need a good dictionary, a stack of identical-sized pieces of paper, and several pens and pencils.

The word setter selects a word from the dictionary and writes out the definition. (If any player is familiar with the word they should say so at the start so another word can be chosen.)

The other players write out a made-up definition on their piece of paper and hand it in to the word setter. At this point the word setter should read through all the definitions to make sure that he or she can read them without stumbling or messing up – anything that would indicate that the definition is someone else's. Then the word setter reads out all the definitions and each of the players announces which one he or she believes is correct. To make it more amusing, you might ask the players to justify their answers.

One point is awarded to each player who gets the definition correct; and also if another player guesses the fake definition you have created; if no player gets the correct definition the word setter gets three points. The 'chair' position of word setter is passed to the next player. When one player has reached an agreed number of points, you have a winner.

Derivatives

Players are given a pencil and some paper. One player chooses a long word and the others all try to make as many words as possible from its letters. The letters may only be used the same number of times they appear in the original word. This game can be played competitively among all players or collectively with all players chipping in with suggestions of their own – a good solution if there are younger children playing.

Great for long train journeys as well as rainy afternoons.

Doublets

Doublets is a word game invented by Lewis Carroll which made its first appearance in *Vanity Fair* in 1879. He described it himself like this:

The rules of the Puzzle are simple enough. Two words are proposed, of the same length; and the Puzzle consists in linking these together by interposing other words, each of which shall differ from the next word in one letter only. That is to say, one letter may be changed in one of the given words, then one letter in the word so obtained, and so on, till we arrive at the other given word. The letters must not be interchanged among themselves, but each must keep to its own place. As an example, the word 'head' may be changed into 'tail' by interposing the words 'heal, teal, tell, tall'. I call the given words 'a Doublet', the interposed words 'Links', and the entire series 'a Chain', of which I here append an example:

H	E	A	D
h	e	a	l
t	e	a	l
t	e	l	l
t	a	l	l
T	A	I	L

It is, perhaps, needless to state that it is de rigueur that the links should be English words, such as might be used in good society.

Here are some more Doublets to try. Write them out on a new piece of paper for players to solve. Solutions at the back of the book.

Get DOOR to LOCK (3 links).
Obtain LOAN from BANK (4 links).
Turn WHEAT into BREAD (6 links).
Turn APE into MAN (4 links).
Turn RICH into POOR (5 links).

You can, of course, invent your own and the challenge is to see who can change one word into the Doublet in the fastest time.

Numerology

The aim of this simple word game is to make words using letters with the biggest number value. Sounds complicated, but read on …

Each person has a sheet of paper and a pen. They write out the alphabet, and underneath number each letter from 1 to 26. So 'A' is 1 and 'Z' is 26. Each player takes it in turn to nominate a category, so the first might decide Vegetables, for example.

The players must choose a vegetable name which will create the highest-scoring word – each letter can only be counted once. So, for example, longer words are likely to score higher, as are words containing any of the letters from the end of the alphabet.

TOMATO = 49 (letters 'T' and 'O' count only once)
CUCUMBER = 62

ARTICHOKE = 90
LETTUCE = 61
AUBERGINE = 77

Buried Names

Players decide between themselves on a category of names. This
might be famous sports personalities or singers, or towns or rivers.
Now each player has five minutes to write a sentence with the name
'buried' in it by breaking up the name and attaching the parts to
different words.

For instance, if the name chosen is 'David Beckham', then the
sentence might read, 'One DAy I was watching a VIDeo when I was
BECKoned into the kitchen by my mum, who asked if I wanted a
cheese or HAM sandwich.' Don't worry about getting all the letters
from the name into the sentence, as long as the parts can be clearly
heard. Also if you can put together a sentence where the parts of the
name are out of sequence, then this will make it more of a challenge!
The sentences are read out and the other players have to try to guess
the buried name.

Acrostics

These can be great fun for all ages – the level of complexity can vary
hugely depending on your age and verbal dexterity. Simply, acrostics
can be any multi-lined piece of writing in which the initial letters
of each line spell out a word or a message. You can make the lines
rhyme if you want – it's more challenging if you do. One of the
most famous acrostics appears in *Alice Through the Looking Glass*:

A boat, beneath a sunny sky
Lingering onward dreamily
In an evening of July –

Children three that nestle near,
Eager eye and willing ear,
Pleased a simple tale to hear –

Long has paled that sunny sky:
Echoes fade and memories die:
Autumn frosts have slain July.

Still she haunts me, phantomwise,
Alice moving under skies
Never seen by waking eyes.

Children yet, the tale to hear,
Eager eye and willing ear,
Lovingly shall nestle near.

In a Wonderland they lie,
Dreaming as the days go by,
Dreaming as the summers die:

Ever drifting down the stream –
Lingering in the golden gleam –
Life, what is it but a dream?

The initial letters of course spell out the real Alice's name, Alice Pleasance Liddell.

You can play this a number of ways. The simplest is probably to suggest the name of someone in the room that everyone tackles as the 'message' spelled out. So, for example, say it is your Aunt Florence, then you might start with: Affable, Untidy, Nice, Tireless, and so on. The words chosen can be as polite or as risqué as you want, depending on who you are playing with.

For younger children the name of a best friend, a pet or their favourite food might be a starting point, Ice Cream or Chocolate, for example. Another popular way is for each player to set a quiz in a certain subject area (History, Geography etc.) the answers to which make an acrostic.

It is an enjoyable enough challenge to play by yourself but it's more fun if you have other people's work to compare with. There are more difficult variations, as you'd expect.

Variation: If you want to make it more challenging, try Double Acrostics in which the start and end letters have to spell out a word – it can be the same word (sometimes with the spelling reversed so it reads from bottom to top) or sometimes it spells another word associated with the first word. Apparently Queen Victoria was fond of this particular kind. It is alleged but not substantiated that she created the following double acrostic:

A city in Italy	NapleS
A river in Germany	ElbE
A town in the United States	WashingtoN
A town in North America	CincinnatI
A town in Holland	AmsterdaM
The Turkish name for Constantinople	StambouL
A town in Bothnia [Lapland]	TorneA
A city in Greece	LepantO
A circle on the globe	EclipticC

Newspaper Alphabet

One player combs through a newspaper or book and writes down
the first word he or she finds beginning with A, then B, and so
on. The remaining players write down the words as they are read
out, and then have a minute to make an intelligible sentence out of
the words thus collected. This can be played in teams or individually.
For sanity's sake don't include the letters X or Z.

Alphabet Race

This is a home-made version of Scrabble™ – with a little twist. One
player draws a ten-by-ten grid for the board. Next each player writes
out the alphabet on a piece of paper, adding three extra As, Es and Is
– these are their playing letters. The aim of the game is to fill the
grid in (turn by turn) with words made up from the player's alphabet
in front of them.

So, for example, say one player writes in Z-E-A-L; he or she
crosses off each of these letters and may not use them again. The
words made must intersect like Scrabble on the board. Whichever
player uses up all his or her letters first is the winner. This is not easy
to achieve, so you might want to impose a time limit, or agree that
when players can no longer contribute a word to the grid, then the
player with the fewest letters left is the winner!

It's a great game to get the creative brain cells racing.

Crossword Puzzles

A variation on Alphabet Race is for each player to draw a five-by-
five grid. Players take it in turns to call out letters which are written
by all players into their grid wherever they choose – the aim of the
game is to fill the grid with as many 'real' words as possible. The
same letters may be called more than once.

Once the grid is full (i.e. Twenty-five letters have been called out) players score the words they have made: five points for a five-letter word; four for a four-letter word and so on. Words within words don't count.

If a letter is called and a player cannot make use of it he or she must quickly put it in the grid regardless. The point is that all players use the same letters to make words.

Orphan Words

This is a fun, quick and creative game for all ages from about six upwards. Randomly select six words: taking the first words from six random pages in a book is as good a way as any. Each player has fifteen minutes to construct a paragraph which incorporates all of the words in as funny or bizarre a way as possible – while still making sense, of course!

Expanding Words

The difficulty with this game is actually in the set-up rather than the deciphering of the puzzle. Each player has to construct a paragraph with, say, six blanks. The blanks represent words of increasing length, each one of which uses all the letters of the previous one but with a letter added. So, for example, *at, tea, late, stale, alters, relates.*

Allow fifteen minutes to half an hour for each player to construct a paragraph. Then each paragraph is read out in turn and the other players have to figure out the missing words.

A Flower Game

Players write down the names of as many flowers beginning with the same letter as they can think up. After five minutes, papers are exchanged and common flowers are crossed off until the winner with the most 'rare' flowers is found.

Variation: The game can be played with any number of categories of words: animals, vegetables, girls' names, and so on.

Word Making

The players all have a pen and paper. Each player has to write down as many words which begin and end with the same letter as they can. The winner is the player with the most words.

Spoken Word Games

Buzz
In this simple game, players must count to one hundred, but with the catch that any time the number seven occurs, or a multiple of seven, they say 'buzz' instead.

Players sit in a circle and the first starts to count by saying 'one', the next player says 'two' and so on, until the seventh player, who says 'buzz'. And each time a multiple of seven is reached, the player must shout the word 'buzz' instead of the number. If anyone forgets and says 'seven', 'fourteen', 'twenty-one', etc. They are out. This game should be played quite quickly so there is not too much time to think about it.

Fizz Buzz
Once you have mastered Buzz, why not try Fizz Buzz? This is exactly the same game but, in addition to saying 'buzz' for the number seven and its multiples, you have to say 'fizz' for nine and multiples of nine as well.

Flower Power
This game needs at least four people to be really effective, and to get maximum enjoyment it should be played at maximum speed.

The players should split into two rows facing each other, either on chairs, or sitting on the floor. The first player on row A calls out the name of a flower, and then the first player on row B should immediately call out the name of a different flower. Then the second player on row A should call out yet another flower name and so on, until either a name is repeated, or the next player hesitates for longer than a couple of seconds. When either of these things happens, the other team scores a point. Agree a total to play towards – maybe fifteen for flower names.

This game is great if played with endless variations on possible categories too. Here are some suggestions: vegetables, countries, trades, drinks, boys' names/girls' names, fruits, animals, birds, capital cities, trees, cars.

Wordy People
Each player is given a letter – maybe drawing from a bag of Scrabble tiles containing no duplicates, or from a pile of paper squares with

letters on them. They then have to say as many words beginning with that letter as they can in a minute. A nominated referee counts the words and tallies the scores – the player with the highest word count wins.

Derivatives and proper names are not allowed, so a player with the letter P may say 'player', but not then 'playing', 'played' or 'plays', and they may not say 'Peter', 'Paul' or 'Peterborough'.

Tongue Twisters

The moment you try to speed through your first tongue twister is the moment when you really start to appreciate the joy and oddness of language. Tongue twisters combine the physical challenge of getting intelligible words out with delight in the nonsense in the phrase being said. Tongue twisters also make great forfeits.

The Guinness Book of Records reckons that the hardest tongue twister is '*The sixth sick sheikh's sixth sheep's sick*' which, to be honest, we don't even think is worth having a go at; there is, however, another camp that claims the toughest is '*The seething sea ceaseth and thus the seething sea sufficeth us*'. Again attempt at your peril. Great fun for livening up a quiet dinner party or on long journeys.

7th November is International Tongue Twister Day, if you're interested in mastering these oral obstacles competitively. And what follows is a short selection of our favourites.

Peter Piper picked a peck of pickled peppers.
A peck of pickled peppers Peter Piper picked.
If Peter Piper picked a peck of pickled peppers,
Where's the peck of pickled peppers Peter Piper picked?

Through three cheese trees three free fleas flew.
While these fleas flew, freezy breeze blew.
Freezy breeze made these three trees freeze.
Freezy trees made these trees' cheese freeze.
That's what made these three free fleas sneeze

From *Fox in Sox* by Dr Seuss

The thirty-three thieves thought that they thrilled the throne throughout Thursday.

Red lorry, yellow lorry, red lorry, yellow lorry.

Eleven benevolent elephants.

Six sleek swans swam swiftly southwards.

How much wood could Chuck Woods' woodchuck chuck, if Chuck Woods' woodchuck could and would chuck wood? If Chuck Woods' woodchuck could and would chuck wood, how much wood could and would Chuck Woods' woodchuck chuck? Chuck Woods' woodchuck would chuck, he would, as much as he could, and chuck as much wood as any woodchuck would, if a woodchuck could and would chuck wood.

I saw Susie sitting in a shoeshine shop.
Where she sits she shines, and where she shines she sits.

I wish to wash my Irish wristwatch.

Fat frogs flying past fast.

She sells seashells on the seashore.
The shells she sells are seashells, I'm sure.

A skunk sat on a stump and thunk the stump stunk, but the stump thunk the skunk stunk.

Our grandmother Daisy taught us this potentially dangerous one:

I'm not the pheasant plucker,
I'm the pheasant plucker's mate.
I'm only plucking pheasants
'Cause the pheasant plucker's late.

Chains

The first player says the name of a town, and then the second player has to say the name of a town beginning with the last letter of the first town. So, player one might say 'Bristol', player two might then say 'Leeds', player three, 'Sheffield', and so on. The game gets increasingly difficult, as no towns may be repeated. Any player who fails or hesitates too long three times is out. Then a variation may be played, a Flower Chain, a Fruit Chain, an Animal Chain or a Country Chain, for example.

Variation: Use the last syllable of a word as the start of a word chain, rather than the last letter of each word. So it might go, 'begin', 'informed', 'medical', 'calculator', and so on.

This is quite a difficult game to keep going, so it is probably suitable for older players. You might want to allow a little thinking time too. Only a little, though.

Conversations

This is another variation on Chains. Players must begin a sentence in a conversation with consecutive letters of the alphabet. So player A might say, 'Awfully rotten weather we're having, isn't it?' To which player two might reply, 'Bad as I've ever known it.' Player three could retort, 'Can't say I find it THAT unpleasant,' and so on.

Not a particularly difficult game, but a good chance to air those acting skills.

The Alphabet Game

The first player must think of a four-word sentence, where each word begins with the letter A – 'Andrew asked Annie afterwards.' The second player must then think of a sentence where each word begins with the letter B, and so on through the alphabet.

If a player fails to think of a (reasonably) sensible sentence within ten seconds, they are out of the game.

This can be great fun because there is no guarantee which letter you will end up with as the game progresses and people drop out, so it's difficult to plan ahead, and obviously some letters are much harder than others.

Like virtually all verbal games, it should be played quickly, though you may want to adjust timings depending on the age of the players.

The Minister's Cat

In this game, players also work through the alphabet, this time looking for adjectives to describe 'the minister's cat'. So, starting with the letter A, it might go:

Player one: 'The minister's cat is an angry cat.'
Player two: 'The minister's cat is an awful cat.'
Player three: 'The minister's cat is an artful cat.'

When all the players have each had a turn, they go round again, using an adjective beginning with the letter B:

Player one: 'The minister's cat is a beautiful cat.'

And so on. Players who can't think of a word, or who repeat an adjective, are out.

The Name Game

This game can be played with two or more players – it's better with more than five. The aim is to answer questions using the initial letters of your name, so if your surname begins with Q or Z, you have our sympathy.

Players sit in a circle. The first to go thinks of a question, which should be answerable in two words and allow a range of responses. 'What's your favourite colour?' or 'What music do you prefer?' are examples.

So, for the first question, if your initials are M.T., you might answer 'Mellow Tangerine,' and for the second, if your initials are S.T., 'Steamy Tango.' You get the idea.

Each of the other players in the circle answers in turn. If players can't think of an answer in a reasonable amount of time, they are out. When the question has been answered by all, then the player sitting to the left of the first questioner asks their question and so on.

Poodle

This is another quick-play verbal game where you'll have to keep your wits about you.

Players agree on a small word, like 'on', 'it', 'and', 'of' or 'an', which will be replaced in all answers by the word 'poodle'.

One player is the question master, who runs proceedings and keeps all the other players on their toes. The question master starts by asking the player to the left a random question which they must quickly answer. The question master may interrupt their answer or suddenly switch attention to another player, asking them the same or a different question at any time. The aim is to catch the players out, by getting them to use the substituted word instead of 'poodle', or hesitate for too long in their response.

So, if the substituted word is 'it', the question master might say to player A, 'What was the weather like yesterday?' Player A might respond, 'Poodle was rainy and cold.' The question master might follow up with, 'Didn't it get nicer later on?' to which the answer might be, 'Poodle stayed the same where I was.' Or the question master might switch and ask another player, 'What's your favourite dog?' 'Poodle is a poodle.'

Anyone using the substituted word, or hesitating, has to drop out of the game. The faster the game goes, the more fun it is, and the harder it becomes to remember which word to avoid. The winner is, of course, the last one left.

Towns and Counties

Players divide into two teams – either sitting in rows opposite each other, or at a table, if it's a small group. A player from one side throws a ball into the lap of a player from the other side, while saying the name of a town. The opposing player must respond with the correct name of the county in which the town is situated within five seconds. If they're right, they score a point and take the next turn. If they're wrong, then the first player scores the point and continues.

A couple of variations of this are to name capital cities and the countries they are in, or footballers and the clubs they play for. There are many others which you can use, depending on the players' knowledge of different subjects.

Shop Till You Drop

Each player takes the name of a shop or a business on the high street – fishmonger, butcher, clothes shop, newsagent and others. One player takes the role of narrator, telling a story which involves her or him visiting the different shops. Once in the shop, she says a letter and the person in charge of the shop has to call out the name of an object on sale beginning with that letter. If the shopkeeper produces a suitable item, then the shopper continues to the next shop, and carries on in this manner along the high street.

So, the narrator might say, 'The other day I went to town to do my shopping and the first place I visited was the butcher's shop. There I asked for an L.' The butcher might reply, 'Leg of lamb.' The narrator should mix up easy and hard letters so the next request might be for something beginning with the letter Q.

If the shopkeeper can't think of anything, then the narrator says, 'Unfortunately the shop closed down,' and the shopkeeper is out of the game. The narrator goes on to the next shop and continues her story, going round the shops again and again, if necessary, until there is only one shop left.

I Love My Love

The aim of this game is for each player to supply seven words beginning with the same letter to complete the following sentence, where in this example the letter is A:

'I love my love with an [A] because he/she is [adjective beginning with A]. I hate him with an [A] because he is [adjective beginning with A]. He took me to the [name of a pub beginning with A] and treated me to [food beginning with A] and [drink beginning with A]. His name is [name beginning with A] and he comes from [place beginning with A].'

If the first player to go successfully completes the challenge, then the player to the left must repeat the sentence, but using the letter B, and so on. If a player fails, they drop out until there is a winner. Again, this game should be played at a brisk pace.

(See also the Portmanteau Game and I Went to Town, page 14.)

Travelling Tales

This is a variation of I Love My Love in which the first player says, 'I am going on a journey to [name of a town beginning with A],' and then must complete the sentence including a verb, adjective and noun, all beginning with A. This is an example: 'I am going on a journey to Aldershot, where I shall Applaud Ambidextrous Altarboys.' The second player must then follow with a sentence full of Bs, and so on. If a player fails to include a verb, adjective and noun, then they are out of the game.

Rhyming Questions

Players sit in a circle and one begins by asking his or her neighbour a question. The next player must answer the question with a statement – the first word of which rhymes with the last word of the question.

So player one may ask, 'Where did you go in June last *year*?' Player two might respond, '*Dear* me, I can't remember *where*,' and player three might follow with, '*Fair* to say, your memory's *dim*,' and player four might add, '*Jim* went to Spain, didn't you go too?' This can be a pleasant bit of nonsense which can quickly become hysterically funny, or you can turn it into a competition by counting people out for failing to deliver a rhyme within a set time.

Cheddar Gorge

This is the very simple, very funny game made famous by the Radio
Four quiz show, *I'm Sorry I Haven't a Clue*. Players construct a
sentence by each adding a word in turn, and trying to avoid being
the player supplying an ending. The more ridiculous the sentence
becomes, the better, but it must make (some) sense. If a player
inadvertently provides the ending of a sentence – containing a
subject, verb and object – then they are out. For example:

> Player one: I
> Player two: decided
> Player three: to
> Player four: go
> Player one: for
> Player two: a
> Player three: long
> Player four: walk

Player four is out because the sentence is complete with a subject (I), a
verb (decided, go) and an object (walk). Player four could have stayed
in the game by adding 'and' or giving an adjective such as 'leisurely'.

Just a Minute

Just a Minute was first broadcast by the BBC in 1968 and has been
one of its most enduring and popular panel games. The aim of the
game is for contestants to speak for a minute on a given subject
without hesitation, repetition or deviation.

Points are awarded to any speaker who is challenged incorrectly
and a bonus is given if he or she manages to complete the entire
minute without a correct challenge.

The other players must listen attentively and try to spot a
repetition, hesitation or deviation.

A player who challenges correctly gets a point and takes over the
topic, in turn trying to complete the minute without interruption.

It is best to appoint someone to chair the game as things can get
a little heated. The chairperson keeps the score and the time and
adjudicates on disputes.

The disputes may be frequent particularly as players challenge on
whether the speaker has hesitated.

You should also agree beforehand which words players are allowed
to repeat ('and', 'of', 'it' etc.).

A player accused of deviation should be allowed to justify themselves. It is then up to the chairperson to decide whether the challenge is allowable.

Associations

Like Flower Power (page 228), this very simple but very effective game *must* be played quickly, without hesitation, or it loses its magic. It can be played with three or more players, though the larger the number the better.

The first player calls out a word – any word – and the player to the left says the first associated word that comes into his or her head, and so on.

So, player one might say 'house', player two 'window', player three 'glass'.

Hesitation, or failure to come up with an association, leads to a player being out.

A player's 'association' can also be challenged. If the group decides that the association is dubious, then the player challenged is out of the game. If the group decides that the challenge is not valid, there is no punishment for the challenger.

Culture Chains

This is a lovely version of Associations for older children and adults with a reasonable knowledge of film, book, TV, song and play titles. One player starts proceedings with the name of a film, book, song or play. The next player in the circle must quickly respond with an associated title. These can be as obscure or witty as you like, as long as a genuine association can be proved. It may be a similar title, a shared author or star, or even just a cunning bit of wordplay.

So, *The Bridge on the River Kwai* might be linked to *Smiley's People*, because they both star Alec Guinness, or to *A Passage to India*, because they were both directed by David Lean or, at a push, *Cry [Kwai] Me a River*, because of the similar-sounding names! If you were really clever, you might say *The Bridge OVER the River Kwai*, because that is the name of the book on which the film was based.

Players must come up with an answer within a reasonable time limit, and the other players must collectively rule on whether the associations are allowable – this game is guaranteed to cause lots of good-natured arguments, as long as it's played in the right spirit.

Codes and Ciphers

I am fairly familiar with all forms of secret writings, and am myself the author of a trifling monograph upon the subject, in which I analyse one hundred and sixty separate ciphers, but I confess that this is entirely new to me. The object of those who invented the system has apparently been to conceal that these characters convey a message, and to give the idea that they are the mere random sketches of children.

Having once recognised, however, that the symbols stood for letters, and having applied the rules which guide us in all forms of secret writings, the solution was easy enough.

Sherlock Holmes, *The Adventure of the Dancing Men*

Here's the code that Holmes cracks …

The message when deciphered read: AM HERE ABE SLANEY (the flags held by some of the dancing men indicated the end of a word).

Codes and ciphers have been around since writing was first invented. In British history perhaps the most infamous use of the dark art of encryption was Mary Queen of Scots who used what is called a 'nomenclature' to try to plot the assassination of Elizabeth I. (See below.)

What's the difference between a code and a cipher?

A code uses complete words or phrases as its base: so each word or phrase that you see represents a complete word; whereas the individual letters are the building blocks for a cipher. One way of thinking of it is that cracking a code is like using a dictionary – you look up distinct blocks of text (or numbers) to find its meaning whereas in a cipher you would have to look each letter up. Hence you need a codebook to send or read a code but in a cipher you need to work out what each individual letter, number or symbol represents.

Here are some common methods of encrypting messages, starting with the easiest.

Word Reverse

At its very simplest, code making can be done by crudely manipulating the words you have to hand. The most obvious way is reversing the letters in a word. So, for example:

WATCH OUT FOR SIMON

becomes:

NOMISROFTUOHCTAW.

It is usual to write this code as a single block.

Every Second Letter

Another simple code that requires you to intersperse each letter of your phrase with a random other letter. It is best to keep this restricted to letters as by using numbers or other symbols you simply highlight the real letters of the message. So, for example:

HDESRWEHCNOXMKETSLMOAURDTFIGN
AEGVLEPRRYSBFOHDBYMHZIQDJEU!

is revealed as:

HERE COMES MARTIN EVERYBODY HIDE!

Code Stick

This method of concealing a message was used by the Ancient Greeks – it was particularly favoured by the Spartans. They used strips of leather wrapped around wooden batons, but nowadays it's easier to use a piece of paper and a pencil.

Take a long strip of paper – about 1cm wide – and wrap it around a pencil so that the edge of each new turn matches up with the edge of the previous turn. Secure the paper at each end with tape. Now simply write your message along the length of the pencil as in the illustration below – if the message is longer than the length of the pencil simply turn the pencil one notch so a new line is exposed and continue writing. Remove the tape once you have finished and remove the paper from the pencil. For the intended recipient of the code to be able to decipher it, all she has to have is a pencil of exactly the same diameter. She wraps the paper around the pencil and reads the message. Without the pencil the message just looks like a random selection of letters.

Number Substitution

This is the classic example of a cipher. In it the person creating the message uses an agreed substitution formula with the recipient of the message. So they might agree that each letter of the alphabet will be replaced by a sequential number starting with A=1. So B=2, C=3 and so on. In order to decipher these messages quickly, writing out a simple grid helps:

A	B	C	D	E	F	G	H	I	J	K	L	M
1	2	3	4	5	6	7	8	9	10	11	12	13

N	O	P	Q	R	S	T	U	V	W	X	Y	Z
14	15	16	17	18	19	20	21	22	23	24	25	26

Alphabet Reverse

Instead of substituting numbers for letters, you could agree to substitute each letter in a message with a different letter. The simplest formula here is to substitute A for Z, B for Y, C for X etc. Again, writing out a simple table will help decipher the messages quickly.

A	B	C	D	E	F	G	H	I	J	K	L	M	N	O	P	Q	R	S	T	U	V	W	X	Y	Z
Z	Y	X	W	V	U	T	S	R	Q	P	O	N	M	L	K	J	I	H	G	F	E	D	C	B	A

Sliding Scale

To make messages more complex to decipher you can 'move' the corresponding letters of the alphabet in the cipher along several places. So you could make A=B or A=C depending on the number you want to 'slip' by. There's a satisfying deciphering tool which can be easily made with just some card, a protractor and a split pin, as shown in the illustration. Cut out two circles of card, one slightly smaller than the other. Next mark out twenty-six segments on each circle (in practice you can use the smaller one and extend the lines to the larger one when it's placed behind). Write a letter in each of the segments on both wheels and stick a split pin through the middle. Designate one wheel as the 'real' alphabet and move the other wheel the appropriate number of letters along – the number of letters you have agreed to slip. Simply by referring to the real alphabet wheel you can quickly discover the equivalent letter in the coded message.

The Masonic Cipher

No, not another Dan Brown novel. This rather elegant and graphically pleasing cipher is very much easier to use than it appears. Take a noughts and crosses grid and starting with the top left-hand square write two letters (A and B) in each, moving left to right and then down. Once you reach the end (should be with Q and R in the bottom right-hand corner), draw two crossing diagonal lines (see illustration for both) and continue anti-clockwise with S and T etc.

The code is then made up of the lines that surround the letter in question – with the first letter in each box (A, C, E, G etc.) simply drawn as the lines and the second letter (B, D, F etc.) as the lines plus a dot in the middle of the drawn lines. You can vary how you distribute the letters, of

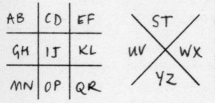

course, as long as you tell your correspondent what you're doing. Using the above code:

HELP ME

looks like this:

$$\rfloor\mathsf{L}\mathsf{E}\mathsf{P}\quad\mathsf{7L}$$

Bletchley Park

This is a two-person game, a paper-and-pen version of the game Mastermind which was very popular in the 1970s/80s. The code setter writes down a four-number combination comprising random numbers from one to nine. The code breaker has ten turns to try to crack the code. He or she first writes down his own random series of four numbers. The code setter marks ticks and dots to the side of the guess – a tick indicating there is a correct number in the correct place and a dot that there is a correct number in the wrong place. Using this information, the code breaker has another go at working out the sequence and this attempt is marked in the same way. And so on until the code breaker cracks the code or fails in the allotted ten attempts.

This can also be played using counters, tiddlywinks or coloured sweets as the code – though sweets might see the code getting eaten before it's been deciphered, just like in the shadowy world of espionage.

INVISIBLE INK

Time was when in order to make 'invisible ink' and perform other feats of secret messaging you had to procure (probably without your parents' knowledge) things like sulphuric acid, fluorspar, turpentine, iodine, coal dust and all manner of things that are either no longer in most people's houses or are banned by health and safety regulations.

Nowadays you need look no further than the kitchen cupboard to find a number of harmless kitchen ingredients in order to pen your secret messages and codes on a piece of paper.

Lemon Juice Method

Use ordinary lemon juice as your secret ink. To write, dip the wooden end of a paintbrush or the point of a knitting needle in the juice and use it as the pen.

Once you have written your message, allow the paper to dry.

For your recipient to read the invisible message, all they need to do is either simply hold the paper up to the sun (on a very hot day) or, better, to a light bulb. The paper can also be held over a candle (for a particularly mysterious and magical feel) but care must be taken not to allow the paper to singe or catch fire.

The heat causes the lemon juice on the paper to darken and become legible.

If you can't wait for the paper to dry you can also sprinkle salt on the drying ink, allow a minute or so and use a wax crayon to rub over the message.

Baking Soda Method

A 50/50 mix of baking soda and water can be used instead of lemon juice. A nice additional trick with this one is to sprinkle the dried writing with purple grape juice (concentrated) – a chemical reaction between the baking soda and the grape juice causes the paper to change colour, and the secret invisible message to appear.

Riddles

The most famous riddle of all is the riddle of the Sphinx.

'What animal is that which goes upon four legs in the morning, upon two at noon, and upon three at night?'

The price for failing to guess this correctly was to be torn limb from limb. Oedipus eventually solved it by guessing that it was man: who in his infancy (morning of his life) crawled on four legs, in adulthood (noon) on two legs and in old age (at night) used a walking stick. The Sphinx, apparently, enraged at the discovery of her riddle, threw herself from a rock and died.

In Britain, setting and trying to solve riddles goes back at least to Anglo-Saxon times. We are lucky to have *The Exeter Book* which dates from the tenth century and, amongst the most extensive collection of Anglo-Saxon poetry still extant, contains nearly a hundred riddles. These riddles are more elegantly conceived than many modern examples. The tradition of riddling was maintained throughout British literary history – from Chaucer to Shakespeare to

Dickens and well into modern times – and was picked up on by
Tolkien in *The Hobbit*. Below are some examples of very early Old
English riddles from *The Exeter Book* and then some used in *The
Hobbit*. The Victorians too loved nothing better than a good riddle
and there is a good selection of Victorian riddles here. Solutions at
the end of the book.

ANGLO-SAXON RIDDLES

1.

A wonderful warrior exists on earth.
Two dumb creatures make him grow bright between them.
Enemies use him against one another.
His strength is fierce but a woman can tame him.
He will meekly serve both men and women
If they know the trick of looking after him
And feeding him properly.
He makes people happy.
He makes their lives better.
But if they let him grow proud
This ungrateful friend soon turns against them.

2.

When I am alive I do not speak.
Anyone who wants to, takes me captive and cuts off my head.
They bite my bare body
I do no harm to anyone unless they cut me first.
Then I soon make them cry.

3.

My home is not quiet but I am not loud.
The lord has meant us to journey together.
I am faster than he and sometimes stronger,
But he keeps on going for longer.
Sometimes I rest but he runs on.
For as long as I am alive I live in him.
If we part from one another
It is I who will die.

4.

I was abandoned by my mother and father.
I wasn't yet breathing.
A kind woman covered me with clothes,
Kept me and looked after me,
Cuddled me as close as if I had been her own child.
Under that covering I grew and grew.
I was unkind to my adopted brothers and sisters.
This lovely woman fed me
Until I was big enough to set out on my own.
She had fewer of her own dear sons and daughters because she did so.

5.

In battle I rage against wave and wind,
Strive against storm, dive down seeking
A strange homeland, shrouded by the sea.
In the grip of war, I am strong when still;
In battle-rush, rolled and ripped
In flight. Conspiring wind and wave
Would steal my treasure, strip my hold,
But I seize glory with a guardian tail
As the clutch of stones stands hard
Against my strength. Can you guess my name?

6.

Wob is my name twisted about –
I'm a strange creature shaped for battle.
When I bend and the battle-sting snakes
Through my belly, I am primed to drive off
The death-stroke. When my lord and tormentor
Releases my limbs, I am long again,
As laced with slaughter, I spit out
The death-blend I swallowed before.
What whistles from my belly does not easily pass,
And the man who seizes this sudden cup
Pays with his life for the long, last drink.
Unwound I will not obey any man;
Bound tight, I serve. Say what I am.

7.

I saw a wonderful creature carrying
Light plunder between its horns.
Curved lamp of the air, cunningly formed,
It fetched home its booty from the day's raid
And plotted to build in its castle if it could,
A night-chamber brightly adorned.
Then over the east wall came another creature
Well known to earth-dwellers. Wonderful as well,
It seized back its booty and sent the plunderer home
Like an unwilling wanderer. The wretch went west,
Moved morosely and murderously on.
Dust rose to the heavens, dew fell on earth –
Night moved on. Afterwards no one
In the world knew where the wanderer had gone.

8.

A moth ate songs – wolfed words!
That seemed a weird dish – that a worm
Should swallow, dumb thief in the dark,
The songs of a man, his chants of glory,
Their place of strength. That thief-guest
Was no wiser for having swallowed words.

9.

I saw a creature wandering the way:
She was devastating – beautifully adorned.
On the wave a miracle: water turned to bone.

VICTORIAN RIDDLES

10.

'Twas whispered in heaven, 'twas muttered in hell.
And echo caught faintly the sound as it fell;
On the confines of earth 'twas permitted to rest,
And the depths of the ocean its presence confess'd;
'Twill be found in the sphere, when 'tis riven asunder;
'Tis seen in the lightning, and heard in the thunder:
'Twas allotted to man with *his* earliest breath,

It assists at his birth, and attends him in death;
Presides o'er his happiness, honour, and health;
Is the prop of his house, and the end of his wealth.
In the heap of the miser 'tis hoarded with care,
But is sure to be lost in his prodigal heir.
It begins every hope – every wish it must bound;
It prays with the hermit, with monarchs is crowned,
Without it the soldier and seaman may roam,
But woe to the wretch that expels it from home.
In the whispers of conscience 'tis sure to be found,
Nor e'en in the whirlwind of passion is drown'd;
'Twill soften the heart – though deaf to the ear,
'Twill make it acutely and instantly hear;
But in short let it rest; like a beautiful flower,
(Oh breathe on it softly), it dies in an hour.

11.

A word of one syllable, easy and short,
Which reads backwards and forwards the same;
It expresses the sentiments warm from the heart,
And to beauty lays principal claim.

12.

A word there is, five syllables contains,
Take one away, no syllable remains.

13.

The beginning of eternity,
The end of time and space;
The beginning of every end,
And end of every place.

14.

What is the longest and yet the shortest thing in the world,
– the swiftest, and yet the slowest,
– the most divisible and the most extended,
– the least valued and most regretted,
– without which nothing can be done,
– which devours every thing, however small,
and yet gives life and spirits to every object, however great?

15.

I'm found in loss, but not in gain,
If you search there, 'twill be in vain;
I'm found in hour, but not in day:
What I am, perhaps, you now can say.

CHARADES

16.

My first is four-sixths of a step that is long,
My second's a person of state;
My whole is a thing that is known to be wrong,
And is a strong symptom of hate.

17.

My first, if you do, you won't hit;
My next, if you do, you will have it;
My whole, if you do, you won't guess it.

18.

My whole is under my second and surrounds my first.

19.

My first I hope you are, my second I see you are,
and my whole I am sure you are.

CONUNDRUMS

20.

Why is your nose like St Paul's?

21.

What street in London puts you in mind of a tooth which has
pained you for a long time?

22.

Why are feet like olden tales?

23.

What word is that, to which if you add a syllable, it will make it shorter?

24.

What thing is that that is lower with a head, than without one?

25.

What two letters of the alphabet make a philosopher?

26.

What is that which is often brought to table, often cut but never eaten?

RIDDLES FROM *THE HOBBIT*

Tolkien's selection of riddles in *The Hobbit* includes the following which are very much in the Anglo-Saxon spirit:

27.

What has roots as nobody sees,
Is taller than trees
Up, up it goes,
And yet never grows?

28.

Thirty white horses on a red hill,
First they champ,
Then they stamp,
Then they stand still.

29.

An eye in a blue face
Saw an eye in a green face
'That eye is like to this eye,'
Said the first eye.
'But in a low place,
Not in a high place.'

30.

It cannot be seen, cannot be felt,
Cannot be heard, cannot be smelt,
It lies behind stars and under hills
And empty holes it fills,
It comes first and follows after,
Ends life, kills laughter.

31.

A box without hinges, key, or lid,
Yet golden treasure inside is hid.

32.

This thing all things devours:
Birds, beasts, trees, flowers;
Gnaws iron, bites steel;
Grinds hard stones to meal;
Slays kings, ruins town,
And beats high mountain down.

The last 'riddle' Bilbo asks always seemed desperately unfair: 'What have I got in my pocket?' It isn't a riddle at all but he gets away with it and makes off with the ring of power. Bad day all round for Gollum. No wonder he's cross.

Solutions to Word Games, Riddles and Conundrums

Solutions for Doublets (pages 222–223)

D	O	O	R	
b	o	o	r	
b	o	o	k	
l	o	o	k	
L	O	C	K	

B	A	N	K	
b	o	n	k	
b	o	o	k	
l	o	o	k	
l	o	o	n	
L	O	A	N	

W	H	E	A	T
c	h	e	a	t
c	h	e	a	p
c	h	e	e	p
c	r	e	e	p
c	r	e	e	d
b	r	e	e	d
B	R	E	A	D

A	P	E
a	p	t
o	p	t
o	a	t
m	a	t
M	A	N

R	I	C	H
r	i	c	k
r	o	c	k
r	o	o	k
b	o	o	k
b	o	o	r
P	O	O	R

Solution for Acrostics (page 226)

NEWCASTLE
COALMINES

SOLUTIONS TO RIDDLES

Anglo-Saxon Riddles (pages 243–245)
1. Fire
2. An onion
3. A fish in a river
4. A cuckoo
5. An anchor
6. A bow
7. The moon and sun
8. A bookworm
9. An iceberg

Victorian Riddles (pages 245–247)
10. The letter H
11. The eye
12. Monosyllable
13. The letter E
14. Time
15. The letter O

Charades (page 247)
16. Stri-king
17. Mis-take
18. Waist-coat
19. Wel-come

Conundrums (pages 247–248)
20. Because it is made of flesh and blood
21. Long Acre
22. Because they are leg-ends
23. Short (add -er)
24. A pillow
25. Y Z (wise head)
26. A pack of cards

Riddles from *The Hobbit* (pages 248–249)

27. A mountain
28. Teeth
29. 'Sun on the daisies it means,' says Gollum
30. Dark
31. An egg
32. Time

Acknowledgements

Thanks to Rosemary Davidson and Rowan Yapp at Square Peg
for their invaluable enthusiasm, knowledge, patience and games.
To the inimitable Friederike Huber for her outstanding design and
her grace under pressure; Eleanor Crow for the superb illustrations;
copy-editor Mary Chamberlain and eagle-eyed proofreaders
Sarah-Jane Forder and Vanessa Neuling. Thanks also to our agent,
Julian Alexander at LAW, for his always sage advice. We've had lots
of help from friends, family and associates but would particularly
like to thank Dad, Kim, Hannah, Cara, Cathy and Julia for their
ideas and support.

About the Authors

Martin and Simon Toseland are brothers who decided a few years
ago that they could test the limits of fraternal existence by writing
together. Since then they have very successfully worked on writing
projects with amongst others James May, Oz Clarke and Neil
Morrissey. For this collection they have researched games and
pastimes dating back hundreds of years.

Index of Games and Pastimes